LEARN E

MW01254177

GOODWILL'S

Learn English— the Easy Way

Mastering the Basic Ingredients of English

By
Dierdre Wolownick Honnold

GOODWILL PUBLISHING HOUSE®
B-3 RATTAN JYOTI, 18 RAJENDRA PLACE
NEW DELHI-110008 (INDIA)

Published in India by :

GOODWILL PUBLISHING HOUSE®

B-3, Rattan Jyoti, 18 Rajendra Place,
New Delhi–110 008 (INDIA)
Phones : 25820556, 25750801
Fax : 91-11-25764396
E-mail : goodwillpub@vsnl.net
         ylp@bol.net.in
Website : www.goodwillpublishinghouse.com

Printed at :-
B.B. Press
Delhi

For all you who've wished that English were
easier ...

For all teachers of English or ESL/EFL
around the world ...

... and for my students

Special thanks to Charles Honnold
for being an inexhaustible
source of support material;
to Brian Bates for his linguistic input
(with an attitude); to Sherry Trechter
for her incisive comments and suggestions
across the miles and the years; to
Winnie Bachmann for her generous
help in making sure it all made sense;
and to all my students
for teaching me so much about the
English language

TABLE OF CONTENTS

✧ ✧ ✧

THE FIRST STEP:
WHAT'S IN THE KITCHEN?

THE NEXT STEP:
COMBINING THE INGREDIENTS

THE FINAL STEPS:
SETTING A BEAUTIFUL TABLE

TO THE READER

Imagine yourself in a kitchen. A world-famous chef tells you, "The contents of the red box are called fi'h**h**, and the contents of the blue box are called miho**h**. Mix them together like this, stir, and serve." You can follow those directions, like a good little student cook, and at the end you've made something good, but... how do you do it again when the chef has gone home?

That's what happens all too often in school. And that's why you don't know how to duplicate your English teacher's recipes once you're on your own.

This is NOT another grammar book; it's a story book. The story of the English language is a wonderful tale of the blending of languages and cultures, of travel, of wars, of religion and politics and how one civilization influences another. Along the way, as English developed, choices were made. Understanding some of those choices will allow you to master this language that you've spoken for years.

In school, you probably went through several grammar books. And if you're like most people, the result of that experience was probably a fervent wish that your English teacher get caught in a time warp, preferably emerging on the other side of the galaxy. You probably came away from school still unsure - more often than you'd care to admit - which word to use, how to punctuate your writing, how to say what you want to say.

This book is the next step.

English is not as difficult as many people believe. In fact, much of its grammar is very simple, almost mathematical. Think about it: while still young, without any help, you figured out enough about the structure of English to say what you needed to say in an understandable manner. Later, though, after years of grammar classes, you probably wound up with a less-than -complete grasp of the structure you've been using all your life.

There's hope! This book will walk you through the basic structure of the English language, making clear not only how to say something, but the reasons behind each choice. And that's the big difference between this book and all the other grammars available in your bookstore. I won't go into any more grammatical detail than absolutely necessary, but I will delve into the reasons for that structure, by referring to etymology (the origin of words), other languages, deep structure (what a phrase really means), and whatever else I think will help you understand why.

Let's face it: Memorizing grammar rules is how they "taught" you grammar in school- and it simply doesn't work. Since you use grammar each time you open your mouth, rote learning is counter-productive. Understanding why a rule exists and where it came from is the key that will liberate you and allow you to internalize and use the structures you need every time you speak or write.

But don't worry: you don't have to be a linguist to understand these basics. I've written this book for you - someone who wants to know more, but doesn't have the time to take another grammar course (which would probably be just as "productive" as the last ones were, anyway).

Some grammatical terms are necessary, of course; you can't describe a language without them. So you will have to learn the terms in Part I. But let's keep it simple. After all, grammar changes constantly. And there are different types of grammar.

Descriptive grammar simply describes things as they are; prescriptive grammar tells you how they should be. And there's deep structure to keep in mind. They all have their value.

I won't debate here which approach is better, which is more appropriate, which is easier; nor do I claim to be the ultimate authority. My approach is eclectic. I've culled what you need to know from all of these types of grammar, and thrown in liberal sprinklings of linguistics, etymology and logic. The result is simple, straightforward and effective. If you work through this book from beginning to end, doing all the Diagnostics and Practices along the way, you'll join the ranks of all my students who have exclaimed in class, "This is so simple - why didn't they teach us this in school?!".

In fact, they're the reason for this book. Having taught the grammar of five different languages to students of all ages and walks of life for over twenty-five years, I've finally taken the advice of my English students and put some of it on paper. To all those who demanded of me, "It isn't fair - they should teach this in school!", I say, "You're absolutely right." They should. But in the meantime, this book will get you started on the road to being comfortable with the English language.

It's like cooking. If you truly understand what each ingredient does to the mixture in front of you, you'll be able not only to follow established recipes, but also to make up your own.

The goal of this book is to help you understand how the ingredients of English work. Armed with that new understanding, you'll be able to mix them creatively, not only to imitate someone else's cake, but to make stews, pies, salads, and tantalizing desserts of your own. In other words, you'll be in charge of the kitchen!

You can use this book as a general reference, thumbing through to find the topic you need at the moment. But if you begin with the first chapter and work your way through, you will finish with a better understanding of English. So I recommend you begin at the beginning, even if you think it's too easy, and build from there. Remember, you can't make soup if you don't understand how to boil water.

So - bon appetit!

Let's get cooking!

The First Step:

WHAT'S
IN
THE
KITCHEN
?

PART I

The Basic Ingredients

"Basic" sounds deceptively simple. But this is probably the single most important step you take in understanding the English language. Just imagine how your cream-puff filling or your apple pie will taste if you don't know the difference between sugar and salt!

Learn the terms. There aren't many, and without them, you'll be lost later. The goal is to **be able to name all the ingredients in your kitchen and know what they do**. Later, armed with that, you can learn what they do when mixed together (in phrases and sentences). And then, when you decide someday that a letter or a paragraph needs more spice, you'll know exactly what to take off the shelf and where to sprinkle it.

When you finish each Part, do the corresponding **Diagnostic** exercises to see how much you've understood. If you don't get over 80% of a Diagnostic exercise correct, do the **Practice** for that topic before going on to the next section (the Practice exercises in the back of the book expand on the Diagnostics, to offer you more chance to practice each topic). Before proceeding to the next Part of the book, be sure you've laid sufficient foundation by doing all the Diagnostics for the current Part. After all, the most elaborate, breathtaking design on the icing won't be worth much if the cake isn't equally delicious.

❖❖❖

LETTERS and their SOUNDS

♦ 1. VOWELS: A, E, I, O and U (and sometimes Y and W)

Of the 26 letters in the English alphabet, five of them, the **vowels**, are special. These are the letters that give the language its sound; hence the name vowel, which shares a common root with the words vocal and voice. The letters Y and W are called semi-vowels; sometimes they function like vowels.

Since each vowel has a sound, a word can be composed of a single vowel alone (like I or A). This can't happen with...

♦ 2. CONSONANTS: All the other letters

The word consonant means "sounding with" (CON- meaning with, and -SONANT, meaning sounding). Consonants have sound when placed with the vowels, but not by themselves. Consequently, it's impossible to pronounce a word composed only of consonants.

That's why words from other languages sometimes seem impossible to pronounce. Often, they put consonants together without the required vowels (for English words), like the composer's name Drdla, or the Polish word "przemysl" (industry). They look funny to English speakers, because to pronounce them in English you would need more vowels, or sounds, between the consonants.

That brings us to the next exciting part about letters - how they sound:

PRONUNCIATION

You might not think pronunciation has a lot to do with grammar. But it does. It plays an important role in mastering English spelling (not as hard as you've been led to believe!), and can even change parts of speech (more on that later). So let's lay down some general groundwork, which will become more and more useful as we progress.

Every letter has its own particular sound. Some, though, have two or even more (to the great distress of people who try to learn English as a foreign language). **It's Important to understand them all**.

♦ 1. Consonants

– One Letter, One Sound

These are the easy ones. You always know how these letters will sound in a word, like M or Z. Nothing to think about.

– One Letter, More Than One Possible Sound

Many consonants have two sounds. Usually, they're called hard and soft sounds. Compare these words:

	HARD	**SOFT**
S:	sassy	easy {sounds like Z}
F:	fort, sofa, fun	of (sounds like V; to change this to hard F, you must double it: off)

C: cat, panic   receive, ice
G: garden, go, guppy   general, age

Generally, soft consonants are followed by the sounds of **E** or **I**, and hard consonants are followed by the sounds of **A, O** or **U**. More on this in the section on Spelling.

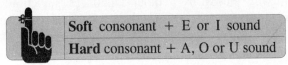

> **Soft** consonant + E or I sound
> **Hard** consonant + A, O or U sound

If you understand this rule of hard and soft consonants, you don't need to memorize some of the spelling rules teachers like to have us commit to memory, like this one:

When a word ends in soft CE or GE, keep the E before "-able" and "-ous."

advantage⇒   advanta**geous**
change   ⇒   chan**geable**
manage   ⇒   mana**geable**

The suffixes -able and -ous begin with hard vowels (A, O and U follow hard consonants}. If you didn't keep the E, the above words would end with the sounds "gus" and "gable." The silent E maintains the soft sound. So this spelling rule **goes without saying**, if you understand the above chart.

You can free your memory of a lot more unnecessary clutter in Part VI, Spelling.

♦ **2. Vowels**

Every vowel in English has at least two pronunciations. These are called long and short, and in the dictionary they're usually represented by the symbols – and ⌣. Compare these sounds:

	LONG –	SHORT
A:	cāpe	căp, ăpple
E:	mēdium	mĕt, bĕt
I:	fīne, bīte	fĭn, bĭt
O:	hōpe, cōne	hŏp, cŏn
U:	ūse, cūte	ŭs, cŭt

Be sure you understand thoroughly the difference between

long and short vowels, because in the chapter on spelling this will be essential.

Every vowel in English also has a third pronunciation, called **schwa**, and this is what causes many spelling errors. Schwa is the sound of any vowel when it's in an unstressed syllable. We say an unstressed syllable quickly, imprecisely, almost skipping over it completely in some cases, and it sounds something like "uh." Here are some examples:

avoid	comp**a**ny	comp**o**sition
fav**o**rite	d**o**zen	def**i**nite

Say these words out loud. In each one, the bold vowel is reduced to a sound resembling "uh." Any vowel can have this sound. Later, in the section on spelling, you'll see how to avoid many of the spelling confusions that arise from this sound.

♦ 3. Diphthongs

That's pronounced "diff-thongs," and it's a very good example of one. A diphthong is a pair of letters that share this peculiarity: when you put them together, they take on a new sound which is sometimes different from that of either of the original letters.

For example, the letter P and the letter H each have a particular sound; but when you put them together, they sound like F (telephone).

Here are some consonant diphthongs:

PH   (sounds like F)
TH   (often represented by the Greek symbol θ in dictionaries)
SH
CH
SI   (SH sound [mission] or ZH sound [vision])

The word "diphthong" has two of them, back to back: PH and TH. Two consonant diphthongs, or more than two consonants together, seem to throw many English speakers into a tizzy! Don't be confused; take them apart and pronounce them separately.

diphthong -	(diph (like F)/ thong)
amphitheater -	("am/fi" - theater, not "ampi"; this is one you'll hear a lot of people mispronounce.)
naphthalene (moth balls) -	(naff - thalene, not 'nap-')

Vowel diphthongs are more pervasive in English. Some sound like one of the two letters combined; some take on a completely different sound. Here are some of the most common; add some of your own to the list:

AI (raise, main)   OO (boot, tooth)
AU (pause, maul)   OA (boat, coat)
EI (their, heir)   OI (loin, noise)
EA (year, eat)   OU (hour, lousy)
IE (chief, believe)

A word about **dieresis.** When two vowels occur next to each other, sometimes you **don't** want them to mel͘ ͘nto a diphthong. Vowel clusters like that have traditionally been written with two dots (called dieresis, or sometimes umlaut, a German word used in English) over the second letter. These two little dots indicate that you should pronounce each of the vowels **separately,** not as one.

coöperation   (not like a chicken **coop**)
reënter   (= to enter again. If you don't use the dieresis, use a hyphen: re-enter. Otherwise, the beginning of the word should sound like "reen.")
preëmpt   (ditto: pre-empt)

This convention, like many others that assist in maintaining clarity, is falling into disuse; but it can drastically affect the pronunciation of the word, so don't be afraid to use it. You want your words to be clear; after all, the purpose of language is to communicate. If little tools like the umlaut can help make it clearer, then use them!

DIAGNOSTICS

Each of these diagnostic exercises will help you determine whether you've understood the preceding information. Do each one as you finish reading the corresponding section. If you score at least 80% correct on each Diagnostic, you can skip the Practices in the back of the book, but they're recommended anyway, to reinforce and help solidify what you've learned. Answers begin on page 140.

PART I

✎ 1: Consonants

Write **H** if the **bold-faced** letter is hard, and S if it's soft.

1. clo**ck** __	6. mana**g**e __	11. pi**c**nic __	16. **f**ool __
2. **g**rand __	7. re**c**eive __	12. **s**inister __	17. mi**s**er __
3. pa**g**e __	8. e**ss**ay __	13. re**s**ilient __	18. a**g**o __
4. **g**um __	9. vi**s**ible __	14. indi**g**o __	19. ea**s**y __
5. **c**ar __	10. **s**imilar __	15. **j**iffy __	20. **g**yrate __

✎ 2: Vowels

Write **L** if the **bold-faced** vowel is long, and S if it's short.

1. c**o**py __	4. p**o**lo __	7. **a**buse __	9. b**e**dding __
2. **i**magine __	5. m**i**ne __	8. **a**bility __	10. r**e**play __
3. c**a**ge __	6. m**i**neral __		

✎ 3: Vowels

Underline the vowel that's pronounced with the "schwa" sound.

1. chocolate	6. magazine	11. gelatin
2. correction	7. ability	12. probability
3. telephone	8. telepathically	13. larceny
4. impeccable	9. protozoa	14. segregation
5. organ	10. metronome	15. chronological

DIAGNOSTICS

✎ 4: Diphthongs

Underline the diphthong in each of the following words, and write **C** if it's a consonant or **V** if it's a vowel. (There may be more than one.)

1. mealtime	___	9. poolhall	___
2. alphabet	___	10. unbelievable	___
3. impeach	___	11. entertainment	___
4. hourglass	___	12. congealed	___
5. anthem	___	13. auditory	___
6. crushing	___	14. ashen	___
7. reproach	___	15. proud	___
8. sharpening	___		

✎ 5: Vowels

Underline all vowel sounds in the following passage, and indicate whether each one is pronounced with a long or short vowel sound, a schwa, or a diphthong.

Pronunciation is a tricky thing in English. You probably know a lot of it without thinking about it, but the rest bears study. When you've mastered the sounds of the letters, you'll be ready to go on to the next section of the book.

PART II

What's that Called, and How does it Taste?

PARTS OF SPEECH

Words are the basic ingredients of any sentence. If you understand how they work, you'll be able to put them together effectively. Do you put garlic in your apple pie? Salt in your tea? Adverbs with nouns? Let's define our terms, and see what each type of word does and doesn't do.

✧ ✧ ✧

WORDS, and the JOBS they do

♦ 1. NOUN

The name of a person, place or thing. From the Latin word "nominum", or "name" (hence the word "nominate," to name). There are three types of nouns:

COMMON	PROPER	COLLECTIVE
table	Mrs. Smith	group
shoe	Abraham	committee
wisdom	Sacramento	army
computer	Europe	family
agenda	White House	team

1. Proper nouns are always capitalized.
2. Collective nouns that refer to a group as a unit use a singular verb:

> The army is building a fort.
> My family is coming for Thanksgiving.

However, if it refers to the individuals in the group, rather than the group as a whole, a plural verb can be used:

> The jury are undecided at this point.
> (Each member of the jury cannot decide.)

✧ ✧ ✧

COUNT and MASS NOUNS

Many nouns can be divided into two categories: **count and mass** (or non-count). Count nouns can be counted, mass nouns can't.

COUNT NOUNS	MASS NOUNS
table	air
cup	coffee
teaspoon	sugar
gallon	gasoline

Think of it in terms of counting: can you say "one sand," "two sands"? But be careful in your logic; you can ask for two coffees, but what you really mean (the **deep structure)** is two cups of coffee. Coffee itself, the liquid, can't be counted; it's a mass noun. You don't count grains of sugar: when you ask for two sugars, you're referring to the packets or cubes it comes in. When you compare two gasolines, you're really talking about two types of gasoline. This distinction is important for the section on Adjectives, later in this chapter.

 BE CAREFUL: Many nouns can be either count or mass, depending on how they're used. Compare these :

COUNT	MASS
one lettuce (=one head)	some lettuce (cut, chopped, etc.)
one milk (=one quart, gallon, glass)	milk, some milk, a little milk
one broccoli (=one bunch or one order in a restaurant)	broccoli, some broccoli, not much broccoli

And some nouns change their meaning, depending on whether they're used as count/non-count, or singular/plural:

Count: There's an egg on the table. (one egg)

Non-count: There's egg on the table. (someone ate a scrambled egg and left a mess)

Count: The committee met to discuss the crimes that were plaguing the neighborhood. (several crimes; many crimes)

Non-count: The sheriff came to talk to the club about crime.
(general topic)

BE CAREFUL which word you use to describe a quantity of nouns Number describes count nouns; amount describes mass nouns.

a great number of visitors...	BUT... a great amount of tourism
a small number of particles...	BUT... a small amount of dust
a large amount of information ...	BUT... a large number of brochures
a small amount of money...	BUT... a small number of coins

APPOSITIVE (Noun In Apposition)

When a noun (or noun phrase) immediately follows another noun, giving more information about the first, the second is called the noun in apposition.

Mr. Conway, the teacher, directed the children in the play.

In the above sentence, Mr. Conway and the teacher are the same person. In Latin, **ad-** means next to, and of course, position means place, hence, one noun placed next to another. Here are some more:

Abraham Lincoln, our sixteenth president, was a great
    (noun)   (appositive noun phrase)
speaker.

The Polish word, pantofle, which means slipper, comes
(noun phrase) (noun in apposition)
from the French word, pantoufle
    (noun phrase) (noun in apposition)

Are you familiar with the Ashcan school.
        (noun phrase)
an artistic movement of the early 20th century?
    (appositive noun phrase)

They presented the petition to Benchley,
    (noun)
the president of the group.
    (appositive)

How to Identify a noun. Ask yourself: is this word the name of a person, place, thing or idea?

♦ 2. ARTICLE

A small word that designates a noun. There are only three:

a
an } (indefinite)   **the** (definite)

A (singular only) designates an indefinite or very general item.

"A report" doesn't tell ŷou which report, the topic of the report or anything at all about it.

An is used in place of **a** when the following word begins with a vowel sound (not necessarily a vowel).

an item; **an** hour (a vowel sound, not a vowel); **an** unusual event

> Keeping an animal requires care. (any animal)
> Do you have an eraser? (any eraser will do)

The designates a specific noun. For example, if you say "the report," you refer to a specific one already mentioned. It often implies **previous Information.**

> Do you have the ruler? (the one I borrowed from you before.)
> You can't get in without the card. (the one I gave you yesterday)

Contrast this use of definite and indefinite articles:

Indefinite.   **A** car is parked in the driveway.
> (Who had the nerve? Whose is it? Is someone coming to visit?
> Why is it there when we have to get our car out of the garage? I hope they get a ticket!)

Definite: **The** car is parked in the driveway.
> (Our car. Harry's car. Someone asked where it is. and this is the reply)

When making a generalization, no article is used:
> **Lemons** are sour.
> **Balance is** essential in learning gymnastics.
> That's **life.**

♦ 3. PRONOUN

A small word that takes the place of a noun (pro means "for;" a pronoun stands for, or in place of, a noun). For example, instead of saying "the book," you can say "**It** is on the table." Instead of saying "Mr. Wilson," you can say "**He's** the chairman of the committee." Instead of giving something to the boys and the girls, you can give it to **them.**

First, a case for **CASE:**

In order to fully understand pronouns and all their uses, you must have at least a nodding acquaintance with case. **Case** refers to the **function of a word in a sentence** (more about that in Part IV, Sentences). Here, I'll just list the various cases of pronouns. But - First, the **GRID:**

	Singular	**Plural**
1st person		
2nd person		
3rd person		

Memorize this grid. This is all-important in understanding pronouns, verbs, case and many other important parts of the structure of English.

- **First person** means the person(s) speaking: **I, we.**
- **Second person** means the person(s) I'm speaking to: **you.**
- **Third person** means who or what we're talking about: **he, she it,** or **they.**

Now, the different cases of pronouns, on their own grids:

SUBJECT PRONOUNS
(Subjective, or Nominative, Case)

	Singular	**Plural**
1st person	I	we
2nd person	you (archaic: thou)	you
3rd person	he, she, it, who what	they

OBJECT PRONOUNS
(Objective Case)

	Singular	Plural
1st person	me	us
2nd person	you (archaic: thee)	you
3rd person	him, her, it, whom what	them

POSSESSIVE PRONOUNS
(Possessive Case)

	Singular	Plural
1st person	mine	ours
2nd person	yours (archaic: thine)	yours
3rd person	his, hers, whose	theirs

REFLEXIVE PRONOUNS

	Singular	Plural
1st person	myself	ourselves
2nd person	yourself (archaic: thyself)	yourselves
3rd person	himself, herself, itself	themselves

And then there are the pronouns that don't fit on the person grid:

DEMONSTRATIVE PRONOUNS
this   that   these   those

RECIPROCAL PRONOUNS
each other   one another

INTERROGATIVE PRONOUNS
who   what   which

Note that these are also listed above, on the Subject and Object grids. I've listed them here separately because they can be either interrogative (a question) or not.

INDEFINITE PRONOUNS

everyone	everybody	everything
someone	somebody	something
anyone	anybody	anything
no one	nobody	nothing
one	some	none
many	both	each
either	neither	more
few	several	all
most	more	some

RELATIVE PRONOUNS

that	which	who	whom

Note: all pronouns that refer to a person are called **Personal Pronouns.**

IMPERSONAL PRONOUNS

it	this	that

These words can refer to specific objects, or to no particular antecedent. Consider this sentence:

It is imperative that they sign the papers by tomorrow.

The word **it** doesn't refer to anything in this sentence. It can be considered an appositive for the noun phrase, that they sign the papers by tomorrow. Or consider this sentence:

That isn't funny.

Here, the word that refers in a general way to something that happened, or to a situation, etc. It has no stated antecedent, but the speaker and the listener know what it refers to.

 How to Identify a pronoun: Ask your-self: Does this word take the place of some noun or noun phrase, whether stated or inferred?

Reprinted with special permission of King Features Syndicate

♦ 4. ADJECTIVE

A word that modifies a noun.

Note: "Modifies" means it tells something about it, describes it, or in some way qualifies or quantifies it. In Latin, "ad" means next to, and "**jacere**" means to lie down or be positioned ("adjacent" means lying, or placed, next to). An adjective is usually placed next to the word it modifies.

(The arrows here, and throughout the book, shows which word modifies which.)

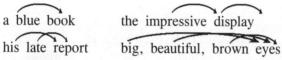

a blue book   the impressive display

his late report   big, beautiful, brown eyes

Remember!! ...an adjective modifies **only** nouns.

Besides their basic, or positive, form, most adjectives have two other forms that you can use for making comparisons:

Positive	Comparative	Superlative
big	bigger	the biggest
lazy	lazier	the laziest
sharp	sharper	the sharpest
loud	louder	the loudest

Adjectives of two or more syllables (a syllable is the smallest unit of sound in a word) add other words to compare them:

intelligent	more intelligent	the most intelligent
unusual	more unusual	the most unusual
interesting	less interesting	the least interesting

(The words **more, most, less and least** are adverbs; more about them in the next section.)

This is a good place to mention a pair of words that many people have trouble with: farther and further. You can see by their endings, "**-er**," that they're both comparisons. But their meaning is different. **Farther** is for distance (measurable); **further** is for extent or amount (intangible).

How much farther is that gas station? (measurable distance)

How much further shall we discuss this? (extent of an intangible: a discussion)

As a little memory tool, consider these comparisons:

| **Distance:far** | **far**ther | **far**thest |
| **Extent:** – | **fur**ther | **fur**thest |

Some adjectives have irregular comparisons:

good	better	the best
bad, ill	worse	the worst
many, much	more	the most
few, little	fewer, less	the fewest, the least

(You've probably heard the expression, "If worse comes to worst ... ", which means, if a situation that has already gotten worse goes one step beyond, to the superlative)

 BE CAREFUL with the last four. **Many** and **few** are used with count nouns only; **much** and **little** are used with non-count, or mass, nouns.

many people, a great **many** things
much water, not **much** water
few facts, very **few** facts
little information, very **little** information

(You'll be understood if you interchange count for non-count forms, but you'll sound a little odd!)

 Notice that the words **few** and **little** are negative words, meaning not many or not much. If you mean them as positive words, use the article **a:**

Negative	**Positive**
few books (meaning "not many")	a few books (meaning "some")
little time (meaning "not much")	a little time (meaning "some")

 Some adjectives have NO comparative or superlative forms, since they express the only possible condition:

Unique (means one of a kind) – Something can be more or less unusual, but it either is or isn't unique: there are no degrees of uniqueness.

Circular - It is or it isn't. If it isn't, it's oval.

Perfect - No matter how close you come, it's not perfect until it's perfect. And once it is, there's no room for improvement.

Some others: pregnant: empty; dead.

To try to compare such adjectives shows you don't under-stand the meaning of the word.

Possessive **Adjectives** look like pronouns: don't be fooled! Remember: a pronoun stands by itself, like a noun (the noun it replaces isn't in the sentence); an adjective always goes with a noun (somewhere in the sentence). Compare these:

ADJECTIVES	PRONOUNS
my	mine
your	yours
his, her,	his, hers, its
our	ours
their	theirs

Examples:

This is **my** house.   This is **mine.**
   (adj)   (pro)

Your salary was docked; **mine** wasn't.
(adj)   (pro)

She checked **his** answers, and he checked **hers.**
         (adj)   (pro)

Their car is on that side of the street; this isn't **theirs.**
(adj)   (pro)

Adjectival Nouns

English has a peculiarity that makes it different from many other languages: it can take one part of speech and simply use it in place of another. An **adjectival noun** is a noun that has been used as an adjective. As languages go, this is unusual, to say the least. Here are some examples :

coffee table   kitchen counter   pocket knife

In each of these expressions, the first word is a noun (coffee, kitchen, pocket), but here each one is being used to describe another noun (table, counter, knife). Without changing them in any way, we simply place them before nouns and they take over the job of adjective.

BORN LOSER reprinted by permission of NEA, Inc.

Adjectival nouns are easy to spot and identify if you think of them the way Romance languages do: by inverting and using a preposition.

Example:

(Fr.) un verre à vin   = a glass for wine (noun)
                           = a wine (adj) glass
(Sp.) el nombre de la **familia** = the name of the family (noun)
                           = the family (adj) name
(It.) I'entrata delia **scuola** = the entrance of the school (noun)
                           = the school (adj) entrance

> **How to identify an adjective:** Ask yourself: Does this word tell me something about a noun that's stated in the sentence, clause or phrase?

♦ 5. ADVERB

A word that modifies a verb, an adjective or another adverb. (For a discussion of verbs, see Section 12, Verb.)

surely	not	more	approximately
soon	less	brightly	now
too	vigorously	then	when
exactly	here	quite	timidly
there	so	merrily	very
always			

... and more examples:

He runs **quickly**   The orchestra played **beautifully**

Their daughter is **extremely** intelligent.

It happened **very** fast.   Press **firmly**

The speech was **not really** appropriate.

Adjectives can be changed into adverbs by adding· -Iy". (The final "y" changes to "i".)

ADJECTIVE		ADVERB
nice	⇒	nicely
happy	⇒	happily
careful	⇒	carefully
fortunate	⇒	fortunately

Some adverbs have a completely different form from their adjective counterpart:

ADJECTIVE		ADVERB
good	⇒	well
ill	⇒	ill, poorly

Like all adjective/adverb pairs, these word pairs have the same general meaning, but their usage is different. Consider these examples:

He's a good singer.   He sings well
   (adj) (noun)   (verb) (adj)

That book is a very good translation of the original.
                  (adj)   (noun)

That book translates the original very well.
        (verb)   (adv)

Adverbs can be categorized according to how they modify the verb. There are adverbs of time (yesterday, today, now, then), adverbs of place (here, there, everywhere), adverbs of manner (subtly, politely, etc.), of quantity (much) – all kinds.

Example:.

The package arrived **yesterday** (adverb of time: when?)

Do it **now!** (adverb of time)

Mr. Howard talks **excessively** (Adverb of quantity: how much?)

They said we should meet them **here.** (adverb of place: where?)

Now that you've studied adjectives and adverbs, you can decide what's wrong with this sign that the author saw on a Nevada State highway:

"Please drive careful."

("Careful" is an adjective; since it modifies "drive" in this sentence, it should be an adverb: Please drive carefully.)

 How to identify an adverb: Ask yourself: Does this word tell me something about a verb, an adjective or another adverb in the sentence?

♦ 6. PREPOSITION

A word that joins the word after it (a noun) to another word in the sentence.

about	at	beyond	inside
past	underneath	above	before
by	like	since	until
across	behind	during	of
through	upto	against	below
except	off	throughout	up
along	beneath	for	on
to	with	among	beside
from	onto	toward	within
around	between	in	over
under	without		

Notice that most prepositions deal with location. **Pre-** means before; **-position** means where something is placed. Prepositions are small words placed **before the noun they link** to the rest of the sentence or clause.

The milk is **on** the table.

Throw it **to** the outfielder.

The noun after the preposition is called the object of the preposition.

(Prep. Phrase)   (Prep. Phrase)

It's in the closet, on the top shelf.

(prep)   (obj)   (prep)   (obj)

How to Identify prepositions:
Think of a squirrel. Now picture a tree. Anywhere that squirrel can go in relation to the tree is a preposition. (Except, of course, for a few like "for," "with," "instead of," etc., which indicate purpose or destination.)

♦ **7. CONJUNCTION**

A word that joins two **similar** elements (that have the same part of speech or construction).

<u>Coffee</u> and <u>tea</u> (joins two nouns)

<u>Red</u> or <u>blue</u> (joins two adjectives)

He wore <u>a plaid jacket</u> but <u>no shirt.</u> (two phrases)

<u>Mom repaired the broken teapot</u> while <u>Dad did the dishes.</u> (two clauses)

<u>We couldn't go to the game</u> because <u>the bank was closed</u> and <u>we didn't have enough money</u>. (three clauses, joined by two conjunctions)

Conjunctions come in two forms:

Simple conjunctions (consist of one word)

after	for	or	unless	whether
and	if	so	until	while
but	nor	till	when	yet

Compound conjunctions

(composed of more than one word)

although	either ... or	neither ... nor
as if	however	not only ... but also
as long as	in-as-much as	whenever
as soon as	in order that	whereas
because		

Con- is from the Latin for "with;" **Junction** means joining. A conjunction joins two or more things of **equal** value. But the key word is **equal.** Don't try to join apples with oranges! Conjunctions link nouns to nouns, verbs to verbs, phrases to phrases, etc.

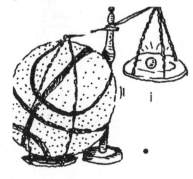

Think of a conjunction as GLUE.

If you try to glue a ping-pong ball to a basketball, you'll wind up with an imbalance. Words exist in balance and harmony with each other.

If you upset the balance, you wind up with gibberish, like:

- Red, blue or a typewriter (adjectives and a noun)
- The cardboard box, and Matilda ate a piece of pie (a noun phrase and a clause).
- I like to read and watching TV. (The conjunction here is used to join an infinitive. 'to read: with a gerund. 'watching'; see 'Verbs' later in this section.

Of course, mistakes with conjunctions aren't usually that obvious. In fact, in speech they're quite common, like this one:

- Because there wasn't time. (The other clause is missing, here you're trying to glue one side of the equation to a missing other side. This is why you learned in school not to begin your sentences with 'because,' It's incomplete.)

But: • Because there wasn't time, we couldn't finish the project. (Here you have both sides of the equation: two clauses. Since they're not in their normal order - clause/ conjunction/clause - you must use a comma.)

 How to Identify a conjunction: Ask yourself: Does this word join two or more similar elements in the sentence?

NOTE: Some of the compound conjunctions can also function in a way that resembles the job of adverbs. Those are sometimes called conjunctive adverbs, and they often express the relation in meaning between the two clauses or sentences. Let's look at an example:

> They were right. However, we decided to ignore their advice.

The word **however** shows the connection in meaning between the two sentences. You could also say that it modifies the whole second clause, or that it modifies the verb **decided.** This is supported by the fact that the conjunctive adverb, much like a real adverb, can be moved:

> We decided, however, to ignore their advice.
> We decided to ignore their advice, however.

Pure conjunctions are more rigid in their placement; they go between clauses. However, for the purpose of punctuation, always remember these words are all conjunctions: if they're out of place (like in the above two sentences), be sure you separate them from the rest of the clause with commas. (See section on commas, p. 99)

♦ 8. INTERJECTION

A word or phrase that interrupts or emphasizes the rest of the sentence. (Also called an expletive; can sometimes stand alone.)

The prefix "inter-" means **between**; the root "-ject" means to **throw**, in Latin. Hence, a word that's thrown into the sentence somewhere, or outside the sentence, for emphasis.

"I did ask you to put it down, but **gosh**, you could have done it more carefully!"

Some common interjections:

Wow!	Oh, ~'\#@+!	Aw,...
Damn!	Gee,...	Hot dog!
Yeeha!	Ah!	Indeed, ...

 How to Identify an Interjection: it's often followed by an exclamation . point. usually expresses strong emotion, and usually functions outside the grammar of the sentence it belongs to.

◆ 9. ROOTS and their AFFIXES

English comes from many languages. Over the centuries, this language that developed first in northern Europe and then in other parts of the world accumulated words, phrases and influences from all over the globe (and is still accumulating them today).

Root means the main part of a word, the part that contains the meaning. The root of a word in English can come from German, French, Sanskrit, Polish, Swahili, Tagalog.... Often, a subtle transformation occurred as the word was adapted into English over the years. Sometimes the root was kept intact. Sometimes it changed, and parts were added at the beginning or the end of the word. These additions are called affixes: if placed at the beginning of a word, it's called a **prefix**, if placed at the end, it's called a **suffix.**

If you look a word up in the dictionary, it's usually divided into syllables. separating the root from the affixes. If you get familiar with the most common roots, especially the ones from Latin and Greek, it will help you figure out new words and handle the ones you already know. Usually a dictionary entry will tell you the meaning first, then give its **derivation** (where the word came from and what its parts meant in that language).

For example, the American Heritage College Dictionary, Third Edition, gives this definition for prefix. "An affix put before a word to produce a derivative or inflected form." Then, it explains where it came from and what those words meant: "Latin **prae** (see pre) + fixer, to place." It goes on to list which parts of the verb were used, and other information about the derivation, ending with a summing up: "prae, pre + figere, to fasten."

It's up to you to make the connections, "Fixer/figere" means to place. So what's a fixture? Something attached in one place. What's a fixation? A consuming interest in one thing (your attention is fixed on that thing). See how it works?

Let's look at some common roots in English and see where they came from and what they mean, so you can figure out new words as you happen upon them. (The hyphens indicate where the root can be joined to its affixes.)

LATIN:

-SPECT-	to see, look. Ex.: inspection (ion = noun; therefore, the act of looking at); spectacle
-SCRIPT-	to write. Ex.: scripture (-ture = noun ending; therefore,act of writing, the writing); description; scribble
-RUPT-	to break Ex.: interrupt (inter=into, between; therefore, to break into a conversation), erupt (break out), rupture.
-VIS-	to see, be seen. Ex.: vision; visible; visibility
-GRADE-	step. Ex.: gradient; graduation (moving to the next step)

GREEK:

-GRAPH-	writing, chart, picture. Ex.: graphologist (one who studies handwriting); biography (bio = life, therefore, writing or story about one's life); geography (geo = earth, therefore, charting or making a picture of the earth)
-CHRON-	time. Ex.: chronicle (story of events in the order they occurred); chronometer (machine to measure time)
-POLIS-	city Ex.: metropolis; politician (man who serves his city)

... and so on. English is filled with words built on roots from other languages, so the more familiar with them you get, the better your command of English will be. You don't need to study the languages; all you need is a good English-language dictionary. Here are a few more you'll want to look up and become familiar with: **aud-, cap-, -pel, -vert, -ject, -scient**... Settle down with a good dictionary and come up with some of your own!

Word Families

Once you know some of the roots, get familiar with the families of words. Many roots have families of words built on them. An example is the root -**gress**, as in progress, ingress, egress, progression, aggression.

-Gress means to go, to walk, to advance. Pro- means forward; so progress means going forward. Re- means back, so regression means moving backward. E- (short for ex-) means out of, so egress means exit. What do you think ingress means?

One more, to get you in the habit: the root -plete comes from the Latin word that means "to fill". What about:

complete?	(Com- means with, so something that's complete is filled up with whatever you're talking about.)
replete?	(Re- means again, so something replete is so full it feels twice filled. This also gives us the verb "replenish," to fill again.)
expletive?	(Ex- means out of, so an expletive functions outside of the rest of the sentence.)

Words in the same family can change their part of speech by adding an affix (another syllable; see next section). This is very common, and if you get familiar with the meanings of the prefixes and suffixes, this will help you decipher new words you encounter. For example, let's start with a verb (see Verbs, p. 46):

Verb: succeed
Noun: success, succession, successful, successive, unsuccessful
Adverb: successfully, successively, unsuccessfully.

As you can see, knowing the prefixes and suffixes can make all the difference between understanding a new word and just seeing a confusion of unrelated letters. (It can also help your spelling; more on that later.)

Now let's start with a noun:

Noun   : power
Verb   : power (up), empower
Adjective : powerful, all-powerful
Adverb   : powerfully, etc.

This is a word game that's worth the time! Let's go through the alphabet and look at a few more, just so you get the hang of how this game is played:

able, unable, disabled (Adj); ability, inability, disability (N); enable (V)

cause (V); causal, causative (Adj); because (Conj)

danger (N); dangerous (Adj); dangerously (Adv); endanger (V)

depend (V); dependence (N); dependable, undependable. dependent, independent (Adj); dependability, undependability, independence (N) dependably, independently (Adv)

final, finite (Adj); finally, infinitely (Adv); finality, finiteness, infinity (N)

forget (V); forgetful, forgotten (Adj); forgettable, unforgettable (Adj)

grace (N); graceful, gracious, ungraceful, graceless (Adj); gracefully, graciously (Adv)

humble (Adj); humble, humiliate (V); humility, humiliation (N); humbly (Adv)

joke (N, V); joker (N); jocular (Adj); jocularity (N); jokingly (Adv)

light (N, Adj); lighting (N); lightly (Adv); lighten, enlighten (V)

manner (N); mannered, mannerless, mannerly, unmannered (Adj); mannerism (N)

maxim, maximum (N); maximum, maximal (Adj); maximize (V)

nurse, nurture (V); nurse, nurse-maid, nurturer, nursery. nursing (N)

press, impress. repress, depress, express (V); press. pressure, impression. expressiveness (N); pressed. impressed, impressive, depressing (Adj)

recognize (V); recognition, reconnaissance (N); recognizable, unrecognizable (Adj)

right (N, Adj); rightful, righteous (Adv); rightfully, righteously (Adv)

similar, dissimilar (Adj); similarity, simile (N); similarly (Adv)

taste (N, V); tasty, tasteful,· tasteless (Adj); taster (N)

term (N); terminal, terminable, interminable (Adj); terminate (V); terminus, termination (N)

use (V); usable, useful, unuseful, useless (Adj); use, usefulness (N); usefully (Adv)

write (V); Writing, writ (N); written; unwritten (Adj)

And there are families within this larger family, like the words that change their main vowel when their part of speech changes:

Long   ⇒ Lengthen
strong   ⇒ strengthen
live (short i) ⇒ enliven (long i)

So develop the habit of taking words apart to examine their smaller parts. If you look up a word, try to remember what the **root** means. That way, when you come across a new word with that root, you'll be able to guess what it might mean, even though you've never seen it before.

And don't forget to give spelling lots of leeway when dealing with roots. Over the centuries, as words changed, spelling adapted to the changes.

judge / judi (**judg**ment: ad**judi**cate: prejudice)
cinder / cend / cin (in**cen**diary, in**cen**erate)

As you can see, knowing how all these families relate (no pun intended) can help you make sense of what seems a chaotic language. The mind-boggling richness of English vocabulary is not so daunting when you know something about its underlying construction. That's the confidence that studying word roots and affixes can give you.

Now – language detectives, front and center! Let's examine the following affixes to see what they mean, and how they combine with their roots. For each one, try to think of other words that use the same affix.

♦ 10. PREFIX

A short syllable attached to the beginning of a word, which changes either its meaning or part of speech, or both.

Here are some common prefixes. Meanings are in parentheses, followed by examples. See if you can think of others.

anti-	(against) anti-war; anti-hero; antithesis (the idea, or thesis, that's the opposite, or goes against, the previous one)

ante-	(before). ante-Bellum (before the war usually referring to the Civil War); ante-chamber (a room in front of another) ante-meridian (the source of a.m., or before-noon)
con-	(with) consult; connect, conversation, community
de-, dis-	(not) deflate; desensitize, disappear, disembark
geo-	(earth) geography (charting of the earth) geothermal (heat generated inside the earth)
im-, in-	(not) immature, impossible, incredible, ineligible
im-, in-	(into) import (carry into) immerse, intake, innate
im-, em-, in-	(cause). improve (cause betterment), empower, insure; ensure
inter-	(between). international (between nations) inter-collegiate (between two colleges)
intra-	(within). intra-mural sports (within the walls of one college, as opposed to between two colleges)
micro-	(small). microscope (machine for seeing small things), micron
multi-	(many). multi-faceted (many-sided), multi-millionaire
photo-	(light). photography (image made by light); photosensitive (sensitive to light)
pre-	(before) prefix; preamble; pre-natal
post-	(after). post-partum; post-meridian (the source of "p.m.", or after-noon)
re-	(again). reheat; recall; re-activate
retro-	(back). retrospect (looking back in time), retrograde (taking a step back)
un-	(not). uninteresting; uncertain

♦ 11. SUFFIX

A short syllable attached to the end of a word, which changes its meaning or part of speech.

Here are some common suffixes. Try to think of others.

-able	(able to, capable of being-). memorable, irreparable, flammable
-ate	(verb ending). active → activate; initial → initiate
-atory	(adjective ending). migrate → migratory; inflame → inflammatory
-er	(one who). teach → teacher; design → designer
-ial	(adjective ending) biaxial, primordial
-ion	(noun ending; changes another form, usually a verb, to a noun) act → action; decide → decision
-ious, -ive	(adjective endings) rebel → rebellious
-uous,	vacuum → vacuous relate → relative
-iary	incinerate → incendiary
-ism	(a belief or philosophy) monotheism (belief in one God: "mono-"=one, "theo-" = God) Romanticism (philosophy held by the artists who belonged to the Romance school)
-ist	(one who practices an art, science, belief) psychiatrist, artist, humorist
-ity	(noun ending; often changes adjectives to nouns) equal → equality; humid → humidity
-less	(without) weight → weightless; care → careless
-ly	(adverb ending) happy → happily; careful → carefully
-ment	(noun ending, act of) amusement, government, amendment
-ness	(noun ending, also usually affixed to adjectives) happy → happiness; rich → richness
-ology	(the study of) chronology ("Chronos", Greek for "time", and -ology = study of time); geology (study of the earth); gerontology (the study of aging)
-ous	(adjective ending) populous, amorous, famous
-tion	(noun ending) act → action; vis (see) → vision
-ty	(noun ending) eternity, parity, beauty, impunity

When examining words for their roots and affixes, keep in mind that different forms of the same word can come from different languages (and thus, be spelled differently). It helps, of course, if you've studied a foreign language in school, although you can learn all about words and their parts by reading the dictionary .

Take, for example, the word "equal" (an adjective). If you studied Spanish in school, you can recognize the word igual. If you studied Italian, you can see the Italian word uguale. The noun form, "equality," comes from the same roots. But the other adjective form with a slightly different meaning, "egalitarian," takes its root from the French branch of the word (egal) as it evolved through the centuries. What-ever language you study in school will help you in English. You just have to be a detective!

♦ 12. VERB

A word that expresses action (physical, mental or emotional), being or state of being.

I've saved verbs for last, on purpose. The verb is the most complex type of word in the English language. It's the only one that can be a whole sentence all by itself ("Sit!" "Enjoy."), and you can't make a complete sentence without one.

That bears repeating: you can't have a complete sentence in English without a verb.

In this section, Basic Ingredients, we'll just examine verbs for their form. Later, in Part IV Sentences, we'll see how they're used in sentence construction when we put the ingredients together.

A. THREE TYPES OF VERBS

The above definition is a general one. Let's separate verbs into three types, or categories: **1) action verbs, 2) copulative (linking) verbs** and **3) phrasal (two-word) verbs.**

1) **Action** verbs are the easiest to spot in a sentence. They show action, movement, thought, etc.

run   jump   sweep   look

possess	exclaim	initiate	write
fly	think	reminisce	dream

2) **Copulative, or linking,** verbs connect one part of the sentence with another. That is their only job; they don't express any action. You can think of them as an equal sign (=). Some copulative verbs are:

be	look	taste	seem	remain
feel	sound	exist	appear	smell

They can join a noun with the adjective that describes it, like in the following:

The <u>sky</u> is <u>blue</u>.   The <u>weather</u> looks <u>cloudy.</u>
   (noun) = (adj)   (noun)   (adi)

<u>Grammar</u> is <u>essential</u> to good, clear writing.
  (noun)   =   (adj)

<u>He</u> appeared <u>pale and shaken</u>.
(pronoun.   =   (adj)
 same as noun)

or they can join a noun with another noun:

<u>Mr Graves</u> is the <u>teacher</u>   <u>Seeing</u> is <u>believing</u>.
  (noun)   =   (noun)   (noun) = (noun)

 How to Identify a copulative, or linking, verb:
Ask yourself: Is the job of this verb only to join one part of the sentence to another?

Consider this example:

That song is beautiful!

Now say it without the verb at all: "Song beautiful!" Is the meaning clear without the verb? Of course; anyone would know what you meant. In fact, many languages do just that: they don't use a copula at all. The sentence is perfectly clear without it. For example, in Russian, sentences like "I hungry" or "She musician" are common and are considered grammatically correct, since the meaning is clear without the copula: "I = hungry" or "She = musician."

This is an important distinction when putting words together in English. Adjectives modify only nouns (or pronouns), and adverbs modify verbs. But copulas are not true verbs; they show no action. So they're not treated like verbs. **Never use an adverb to modify a copulative verb.**

Consider the following :

The wine tastes good
(noun)   =   (adj)
(Description: it's a good wine; the wine's not doing anything)

The wine-taster tastes well.
(verb)(adverb)
(Action: that's his job. He tastes wine for a living.)

The same word, "tastes," can be either a true verb (action word) or a copula (linking a noun, **wine,** with its description, **good).**

That stew smells wonderful!
(Description: the stew isn't doing anything)

That hound smells terrible (not terribly).
(Description of the odor; no action)

But: That hound smells wonderfully!
(Action: he can sniff out anything; his nose works wonderfully well)

The same word, "smells," can be either a true verb (action word) or a copula (linking a noun, stew, with its description, wonderful). Most of the five sense verbs have 'two forms, true verb and copula:

Copula	Verb
look good (appearance)	See well (action of seeing)
sound good (sound)	hear well (action of listening/hearing)
taste good (culinary description)	taste well (like a wine-taster)
smell good (odor)	smell/sniff/track well (like a hound)
feel good (health, sensation)	feel well (?)

This is what you need to remember the next time you hesitate between saying "I don't feel good" or "I don't feel well." Which do you mean: your state of being (description) or the act of touching or feeling (the tactile sense)? "Good" (the adjective) goes with the description of the noun or pronoun (your condition). "Well" (the adverb) goes with the action of feeling (how well you can feel objects).

But remember, in "To the Reader," that I said grammar changes constantly? This is a good example of that phenomenon. In the last few years, it's become more and more common to hear people say, "I don't feel well" (using the adverb instead of the adjective to describe a noun/pronoun). This usage probably began as an error since adverbs have never been used, historically, to modify nouns; someone mistakenly said "well," thinking it sounded better than "good." And then someone else said it, and someone else ... and it caught on.

That's how grammar changes. That's how English lost its verb forms. If you go back far enough in time, English speakers had to put endings on the verbs, just like they do in Spanish or French (we still have one recognizable, though archaic, form: "-est" as in "thou goest" or "thou hast"). But people stopped using them, little by little, and over the centuries the usage changed. The grammar changed.

In fact, some dictionaries actually list "well" as a synonym (same meaning) for the adjective "healthy," as in "well-baby care" that you see in hospitals and clinics now. In some places, they've even gone so far as to invent the word "wellness," which, as far as I can tell, means good health! But it's generally considered an adverb, so use it as such. If you don't feel good when you study grammar, say so!

3) Phrasal (two-word) verbs

These are verbs that have more than one word, like: look at, listen to, find out, put up (with), get up, look out, put on, carry out, drop by, hand in, etc. Some of these are separable, that is, the verb and its preposition can be separated; some are inseparable.

For example, you can "put on your shirt" or you can "put your shirt on" (separable), but you can't "drop at your friend's house by" (inseparable). You can "look up a word" or you can look a word up," but you can't "listen the beautiful music to."

Here's a partial list of both types. See how many more you can think of:

SEPARABLE	INSEPARABLE
take out	drop by
take over	listen to
hand in, over	fall down
turn up (something)	turn up (to appear)
find out	buy into
foul up	look at
bring up	look for
carry out	

Many phrasal verbs have a one-word counterpart, for example:

get up = rise	mess up, foul up = ruin
put on = don	put together = assemble
takeoff = remove	carry out = execute, realize
find out = discover, learn	

The phrasal verb is usually more colloquial – less formal – than the one-word form. The one-word form is usually the form of choice for writing, and the phrasal verb is the one you'll hear most often in spoken form.

One phrasal verb is special, so we'll look at it separately:

have got = have

Many people use **have got** instead of using the verb **have,** as in **I've got a terrible headache.** Be careful not to confuse this form with the past tense **I've gotten** (see Section E, Auxiliary Verbs).

If you see a preposition closely following a verb in a sentence, check to see if it's a phrasal verb. Say the verb alone out loud. If it's a phrasal verb, it won't make sense without its preposition.

◆ B. INFINITIVE

The name, or title, of a verb, always preceded by "to." Here are some infinitives:

to go	to be
to examine	to do
to illustrate	to swim

An infinitive doesn't function at all like a verb. It's usually a noun, dressed up like a verb.

Example:

To err is human. (The infinitive to err is a noun, subject of the verb is.)

He likes to ski. (to ski is the object of the verb likes.)

 Remember: if you see the word "to" in front of a verb, it's almost always an infinitive.

Let's stop here for a moment and take a visual look at how verbs are put together. Remember the grid from Part II, Pronouns? I said there that all verbs fit on that grid, too, so let's do one and see what it looks like. Let's start with the verb TO BE (when naming a verb, use the infinitive):

TO BE

	Singular	Plural
1st person	I **am**	we **are**
2nd person	you **are**	you **are**
3rd person	he, she, it **is**	they **are**

TO BE is the only verb in English that kept all of its inflected forms (forms with different endings for different persons, like in other languages). Most of the other verbs only kept one inflected form, the 3rd person singular:

TO GO

	Singular	Plural
1st person	I **go**	we **go**
2nd person	you **go**	you **go**
3rd person	he, she, it **goes**	they **go**

This is why it sounds non-standard when you hear people say "don't he?", "you is," "that be," etc. They've put a singular subject with a plural verb, or used an infinitive with a subject. It's like mixing apples and oranges; they just don't go together. In some regions or social groups, such mixing of forms is acceptable. But it is non-standard English. By all means, use such forms to fit in with the group you're with, if that's the regional or social norm; but know that it's not appropriate for more formal audiences.

Placing verbs on this grid to show agreement between subject and verb is called conjugating. Here, we've conjugated two verbs. It's good practice to get in the habit of conjugating verbs in different tenses (see Section G, Tense). This gives you a good "feel" for which forms go with which pronouns, as well as a good general understanding of the verbal construction of English.

◆ **C. GERUND**

The "-ing" form of a verb. Also called a **present participle**. Here are some gerunds:

singing	wishing	hopping	imagining	buying
preparing	doing	closing	being	understanding

More versatile than the infinitive, the gerund can act like a noun or an adjective, or be part of a verb phrase (more on those later).

> My son loves swimming. (gerund used as a noun: he loves what?)
>
> They're building a new house. (part of the main verb "are building")
>
> The whistling wind drove the settlers crazy. (gerund used as an adjective; what kind of wind?)

When a gerund serves as an adjective, as in the above example, it can be called a participle adjective, since another name for a gerund is the present participle; see also page 53 for past participles as adjectives.

Gerunds are always preceded by possessive case pronouns:

✗ I don't understand him refusing to go.

✔ **I don't understand his refusing to go.**

   ✗ She can't stand him singing in the shower.

   ✔ **She can't stand his singing in the shower.**

It's not him she can't stand, it's the singing (a noun). The pronoun form that acts like an adjective before a noun is the possessive.

 If the verb ends with "-ing" it's a gerund (no matter what function that gerund has in its sentence).

♦ D. THREE PRINCIPAL PARTS Of VERBS

Every verb in English has three principal, or main, parts. Categorizing a verb into its parts can help you understand how to use it. You probably know these forms, although you may not be familiar with what they're called. Here are a few; see if you can think of more.

Regular Verbs (add "-ed" to verb)

Present	Simple Past	Past Participle
close	closed	closed
enter	entered	entered
hurry	hurried	hurried
lay (to put, place)	laid	laid
listen	listened	listened
play	played	played

Irregular Verbs

am	was	been
begin	began	begun
break	broke	broken
choose	chose	chosen
come	came	come
do	did	done
draw	drew	drawn
drive	drove	driven
eat	ate	eaten
go	went	gone
lie (to recline)	lay	lain
see	saw	seen

speak	spoke	spoken
swim	swam	swum
write	wrote	written

Past participles combine with auxiliary verbs (see Section G,), to form the past tense, and also can be used as adjectives.

the **written word**
(adj.) (noun)

♦ E. AUXILIARY (HELPING) VERBS

Some verbs, usually to have and to be, are used as helpers in some verb tenses. They don't convey the main meaning of the verb, but only help put the verb in the correct tense (more on verbs and verb tense in Section G).

They **have** spoken. We **had** never seen it.
She's studying German. He **is** come. (Archaic)
They **do** enjoy tennis!

The other verb that conveys the meaning of the action is called the **main verb** (spoken, seen, studying, come, and enjoy in the previous examples).

The auxiliary in the last example, **do,** is the one used in forming questions. Let's take a look at how questions are made:

Forming Questions

— In the Present:

With the verb TO BE and with modals (see **F** below), simply invert subject and verb.

Statement:	**Question:**
He is tall.	is he tall?
Mark can ski.	Can Mark ski?
They aren't here.	Aren't they here?

BUT with other verbs, you must add the auxiliary **DO**, in one of its forms, to make a question:

Statement:	**Question:**
They always pay their bills.	Do they always pay their bills?
She finished the job yesterday.	Did she finish the job?

— In tenses with an auxiliary verb:

Invert the subject and the auxiliary verb.

Statement:	**Question:**
They haven't finished.	Haven't they finished?
It's coming.	Is it coming?
He's already seen it.	Has he already seen it?

— Tag Questions

Often, when we speak, we want our listener to confirm, negate or otherwise respond to what we've said. We can request this information by adding a small tag question at the end of our statement, like this:

You've already studied English, **haven't you?**

Tag questions are very widely used in spoken English, but are not very common in writing. To make a tag question:

If there's a modal or auxiliary in the statement, use only that modal or auxiliary in the tag question (not the main verb):

She **hasn't** seen them in years, **has** she?

I guess I **should** try it, **shouldn't** I?

If there's no modal (see **F**) or auxiliary, use **DO** in one of its forms:

You **took** the train, **didn't** you?

They **speak** Greek at home, **don't** they?

If the statement is negative, make the question positive (and vice-versa):

Carmen **isn't** attending class any more, **is** she?

He**'s** arriving tomorrow, **isn't** he?

NOTE: In a sentence, the auxiliary is the part that must agree with the subject (keep the same person and number). The main verb keeps its unchanged base form.

She speaks.	⇒ Does she speak?
That store sells bagels	⇒ Does it sell bagels?
He speaks Japanese	⇒ He doesn't speak Japanese?

♦ F. MODALS

A modal isn't really a verb. It's a word that helps modulate the verb, that is, helps change its tense or its mood (more on those later).

Here are some common modals:

can	may	will
could	might	would
ought	shall	should

I think it'**ll** rain later. (**will** changes rain to the future tense)

You **should** really study. (**should** is the modal that implies duty)

Would you come if you could?

(**would come** is the conditional mood. implying the condition "if you could")

♦ G. TENSE

The word "tense" in grammar comes from tempus in Latin, meaning time. (The other "tense" comes from the Latin tensus, meaning stretched, taut.) Tense refers to when the action of the verb takes place. Following are examples of all the major tenses in English. Study them to be sure you know exactly how each one is constructed.

VERB TENSES

(Simple) Present   = I speak
(Used for general statements, for repeated actions in the present (like "I get up at six o'clock"), and for present narration. Unlike most other languages, English verbs have no inflected forms – endings – except the third person singular: he speaks. If you fail to use the final -s on this form, your English will sound non-standard, or dialect.)

Present Progressive: = I am speaking
(also called Pres. Continuous)   (action happening while speaker is speaking)

Present (emphatic) :   = I do speak
(for contrast or emphasis: I don't speak Russian, but I do speak Spanish.)

Present Perfect: = I have spoken
(action begun some time unspecified in the past, and completed in the present; "perfect" in Latin means completed.)

Present Perfect Progressive: = I have been speaking
(Pres. Perf. Continuous) (the "perfect" refers to the helping, or auxiliary, verb; action began in past, continued to the present, and is still happening when speaker is speaking.)

(Simple Past (or Preterite):   = I spoke
(one-time action in the past)

Pluperfect (Past Perfect): = I had spoken
(used for an action which occurred before another action in the sentence, to distinguish which is "more past")

Past Progressive :   = I was speaking
(Past Continuous) (shows ongoing action or a description in the past)

Past Perfect Progressive: = I had been speaking
(Past Perf. Continuous) (action begun some time unspecified in the past, and was completed prior to some other past tense in the sentence.)

Future (really a mood):   = I will speak
(express a future action or condition)

Future Progressive: = I will be speaking
(Future Continuous) (an on-going action in the future)

Future Perfect: = I will have spoken
(stresses the completion of an action at a given time in the future)

Future Perfect Progressive: = I will have been speaking
(Fut. Perf. Continuous) (an action that will have been on-going at a given time in the future)

Conditional (really a mood):   = I would speak
(expresses the action that would result if a condition were met; also used to express habitual action in the past.)

Conditional Perfect: = I would have spoken
(action that would have been the result if a condition had been met)

Conditional Perfect Progressive: = I would have been speaking
(Cond. Perf. Continuous) (action that would have been on-going in the future if a condition had been met)

♦ H. TRANSITIVE / INTRANSITIVE VERBS

The word "transit" means travel or transfer, coming from the Latin word that means "to go across;" a transitive verb is one where the action "travels," or crosses, from the subject to the direct object.

He ate an apple.
(Sub) (V) (Dir Obj)

"He" is the one doing the action: the subject. What he's

doing is the **verb**. And what did he eat? The apple, the **direct object** of the verb "ate."

The direct object of a verb always answers the direct question, "what?" or "whom?" about the verb.
A transitive verb has a direct object. An intransitive verb doesn't.

They finished the report in an hour. (transitive)
(Sub) (V.) (Dir Obj)

At lunch, the teacher handed out tests. (transitive)
        (Sub) (V) (Dir Obj)

But: During the break, the teacher and I talked. (Intransitive)
                (Sub)   (V)

Some verbs can be either transitive or intransitive, depending on whether they have a direct object.

They ate dinner. (Trans.; it says what they ate)
    (V) (Dir Obj)

They ate at a restaurant. (Intrans.; it doesn't say what they ate)
    (V)

How do you determine whether a verb is transitive or intransitive? Ask yourself, Does the verb have a direct object? If it does, it's transitive.

Remember: A direct object answers the direct question "what?" or "whom?" about the verb.

♦ I. ACTIVE AND PASSIVE VOICE

The arrangement of the sentence by role (agent/object) is called Voice. Active Voice follows normal word order: S-V-O. Passive Voice starts with the object: O-V-Agent (formerly the subject).

Verbs in the active voice follow the normal word order for an English sentence: Subject - Verb - Object.

<u>Emil Zola</u> <u>wrote</u> <u>many books.</u>
(Sub)   M   (Dir Obj)

But you can change the order of the words, yet still state that same information. Let's see how it looks if you begin with the Object:

<u>Many books</u> <u>were written</u> by <u>Emil Zola.</u>
(Dir Obj)   M   (Agent)

This is a **passive voice** sentence. In this version, the object is stated first. But although the object has taken the usual place of the subject, it's not doing the action (the books aren't writing anything). We can call this new "non-subject" the passive subject. Call it anything you want; just remember that it's **not** the subject, the do-er, of the verb.

The verb now has two words: "were written." Verbs in the passive voice are composed of the helping verb **"to be"** plus the **past participle.**

And the former subject is now called the **agent**, that is, the one really doing the action. Zola still wrote the books. It's preceded by the word "by."

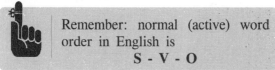

Remember: normal (active) word order in English is
S - V - O

But a word of caution: The **Passive Voice** is usually a very **remote, Impersonal form.** What you've done is 'removed the person responsible for the action from the position of subject of the sentence.' This has the effect of de-personalizing the action.

For this reason, you'll see a lot of passive voice in government documents, legal jargon, business writing, etc., anywhere where the agent (the person or person actually doing the action) doesn't want to be known or seen as directly associated with the action. It has an "official" business-like sound to it.

The crime was reported last night. (but we're not saying by whom)

Taxes were raised in 1994.

(who'd want to be recognized as responsible for that one?!)

The car was struck from the rear. (by the alleged guilty party)

So if you choose to use the passive voice, be sure that that's the effect you want to create. The passive construction is not always so easily recognizable, especially if the sentence is very long. Just remember: normal (active) word order in English is

S - V - O

♦ **J. SUBJUNCTIVE**

The subjunctive is a **mood,** and although mood is covered in **Part IV, Sentences,** we first need to look at the form it takes.

Subjunctive is the mood used when a statement is contrary to fact, or an implied command. In the first case, use the past subjunctive:

I wish **she were** rich. (She's not rich; this Is contrary to fact)

If I **had** time I'd write a book. (I don't have the time)

In the case of implied command, use the present subjunctive:

It is imperative that **he do** it as soon as possible.

Normally. we never say "he do" or "she were" (except in non-standard English). Since English only has one inflected verb form, the 3rd person singular, that's the one that shows the subjunctiveness. Let's look at the two in the present:

to BE		to GO	
I be	we be	I go	we go
you be	you be	you go	you go
he, she, it be	they be	he, she, it go	they go

It's important that **you be** on time.

His parents insisted that **he go** to college.

As you can see, the subjunctive form looks exactly like the infinitive without the "to." The past subjective looks just like the simple past (indicative), except for the verb "to BE:"

to BE		to GO	
I were	we were	I had	we had
you be	you were	you had	you had
he, she, it be	they were	he, she, it had	they had

It would be great if **she were** chosen.

I wish **I were** a millionaire!

If only **he knew** the answer.

I wish **we had** more time.

Generally, the present subjunctive is used for implied commands, and the past subjunctive is used for wishes, hopes, etc., that are contrary to fact. (Speakers of other languages will recognize these constructions, especially those who speak Romance languages.)

Would that **she were** mine! (hope)

(Sp.) !Ojala que fuera la mia!

If only **that were** true! (wishing for something contrary to fact)

(It.) Se fosse vero!

It was essential that **she finish** the project in May. (Implied command) (Fr.) ll est essentiel qu'elle finisse le projet au mois de mai.

They demand that **he obey** their rules. (implied command)

(Fr.) lis exigent qu'il obeisse a leurs regles.

◆ PART II SUMMARY. A SCHEMATIC TABLE

Compatible Parts of Speech

Which parts of speech go with which? If you're sure of that, putting words together (the next Part) will be easier. Here's a chart that shows which words go together.

Part of Speech	What it combines with
Noun	preceded by Article or Adjective; Adjective/Noun can follow, joined by copula
Article	followed by Noun
Pronoun	can be joined to Adjective or Noun by copula; can follow a Preposition
Adjective	Noun or noun phrase
Adverb	Verb; Adjective; other Adverb
Preposition	followed by Noun (phrase) or Pronoun
Conjunction	between any two elements that are of the same part of speech or construction
Interjection	stands alone, or separated from grammatical sentence by punctuation
Verb ● True:	other Verb or modal; Adverb
● Copula:	links subject with Noun (phrase) or Adjective (phrase)

DIAGNOSTICS

PART II

✎ 6: Nouns

Write C for common, P for proper and Cl for collective.

1. chalkboard ___   5. Australia ___   8. Venus ___
2. Paris ___   6. exercise ___   9. the military ___
3. automobile ___   7. family ___   10. Mrs. Cartelli ___
4. committee ___

✎ 7: Nouns

Write C for a count noun and M for a mass (non-count) noun.

1. sugar ___   5. gasoline ___   9. beads ___
2. book ___   6. shoes ___   10. appointment ___
3. air ___   7. beef ___
4. box ___   8. orange juice ___

✎ 8: Nouns

Correct any count/mass nouns used incorrectly. Write C if the sentence is correct as is.

1. The ads for the new toothpaste promised less cavities during your next dental check-up.
2. Dad wanted to know how much of the new stamps you bought.
3. If you want to lose weight, exercise more and consume less calories.
4. In the photo it looks like a lot of people, but actually there were fewer than fifteen members present.
5. Only a little of the people in the auditorium were able to hear the fire bell when it rang.
6. According to last month's statistics, less than seven employees actually met their quota.
7. The player with the greatest amount of points wins.
8. How can that resort afford to stay open? I've never seen so little tourists around this beach.

9. This national park is a place of extremes: one year you can see more species of birds fly over here than at any other park, and the next year year, the least.
10. There were less attendance hours recorded last semester, yet more students went on to the next level than ever before.

✎ 9: Nouns

Underline the <u>noun</u> (or noun phrase) once and its <u>appositive</u> (noun in apposition) twice.

1. Mr. Bukowski, our esteemed colleague, was the man responsible for this new system of accounting.
2. He thought of Uncle Ted, his mentor and teacher, and wished he were there.
3. One of her fondest dreams was to be like Mrs. Fitzpatrick,. her first-grade teacher.
4. I'd always hated studying grammar, a dry, boring set of rules, until I met Mr. Atsuyama, my college English teacher.
5. All the employees in the office got together and wrote a joint, co-signed letter to Harris Forbes, the founder of the magazine that had lambasted their firm.
6. Red, a primary color, makes the flowers in this landscape stand out brilliantly.
7. For their homework, which was usually quite substantial, they only had to look up some facts in Dog Fancy, a magazine devoted to dogs and people who love them.
8. The fact that you didn't finish the job doesn't look good on your resume.
9. Last weekend, I went to a ball-game with my friend Juan.
10. I'll never forget the day I first saw Elsie the Cow, the mascot for Borden's Milk Companyl

✎ 10: Nouns

Draw two lines under each <u>adjective noun</u> and one line under each <u>noun</u>.

1. Where did Mom put the cookie dough?
2. Paper dolls were lying all over the floor, and Katie sat in front of her doll house cutting out more.
3. I didn't feel good, so I went to the store to get some headache medicine.

4. Computer programming is the job of the future.
5. Sabjali Hassam, a newspaper reporter from Madagascar, was working for a year at the New York Times as part of a professional exchange.
6. The highly-paid speaker called their city a cow town, offending all the civic leaders in the conference room.
7. The loud noise startled Millie, causing her to spill the cake mix all over the marble counter top.
8. The door handle fell off in his hands, and his impetus made him topple back onto the porch railing.
9. When the encyclopedia salesman ran down the front steps, chased by the barking dog, he tripped and fell over the garden hose that lay curled up on the lawn.
10. One of the hardiest of all breeds, the Alaskan sled dog often sleeps under a mound of snow that falls on him during the arctic night.

✎ 11: Articles

Underline all articles.

1. It is the decision of the Board that all employees on the Retirement Plan are eligible for an interest-bearing retirement account at a bank of their choice.
2. The platypus is an animal indigenous to Australia.
3. If you mix a half-pound of butter with an ounce of chocolate and a cup of sugar, the result is delicious!
4. Where's the sign-in book? Over there, on the counter.
5. Which is heavier, a pound of feathers or a pound of gold?

✎ 12: Pronouns

Underline all pronouns and indicate person, number and case or type.
Example:
He and **I** are giving a presentation on Friday.
(3rd person, (1st person, sing., sub.)
  sing., sub.)

1. I gave her the books, but somehow they got misplaced.
2. Didn't you see them? They're over there.
3. Look at the puppies; they're playing with each other!
4. Give them to me! They're mine!
5. If it falls, pick it up.

6. The best thing we can do for the world is to love one another.
7. I think something's wrong; it shouldn't sound like that.
8. Do you want these or those?
9. The ones that are in the window go in that box.
10. The project which the company began in September should bring us results by December.

✎ 13: Pronouns

Correct any pronoun errors in the following passage.

"When we arrive at the hotel. Marcia, you and John set up the tables first. Cover it with the linen cloths, white on the bottom and the pink ones on top, laid out on the bias.

"Carmen, you and Mike will take care of setting out the meats. You can each do one table. John can help you when he's finished covering tables. Him and Marcia are just here for the day, so they'll help out wherever they can.

"Vladimir, get them trays of glasses out of the back of the truck; you can set them up in pyramids, like you did at the last job. That was beautiful!

"Anna, once the tables are covered and the casseroles are out, start setting out the rest of the food. You'll have some help from Vladimir and I, once I've finished talking with the bride's mother.

"Now, I want ice around all the cheeses, the soft stuff, all the perishables. Vladimir, you're the one which is responsible for that. Keep that ice coming! When it starts to melt or if people take it for their drinks, keep refilling it."

✎ 14: Adjectives

1) Underline all adjectives. 2) Indicate adjective (A), gerund adjective (G). adjectival noun (AN), possessive adjective (PA) or demonstrative adjective (DA) for each one.

1. Deafening thunder rattled the old house.
2. Come explore the exciting process of planning a summer vacation by car.
3. A remarkable developmental sequence occurs during a baby's early months.
4. This toy is a floor-based activity center, just perfect for little fingers.

5. The amber grain fields swayed and danced under the gentle morning breezes.
6. Where's your little sister?
7. Her coffee mug is on the kitchen table.
8. Ineffective though it may seem at ,times, talking with children is still the best way to re-direct their behavior.
9. When she was little, she always slept with an adorable little pink puppy made of felt and a blue, fuzzy blanket that she called her "Blankie."
10. The surprisingly small garden was overflowing with fresh vegetables-summer squash, ripe, aromatic melons, green and red peppers-and over it all, in one corner, stood a dwarf fruit tree so laden with peaches that it seemed bowed with the effort of supporting it all.

✎ 15: Adverbs

Underline all adverbs.

1. To stay healthy, eat well and exercise often.
2. He raised the gun slowly, took aim carefully and squeezed the trigger.
3. Mahatma Ghandi spoke ill of no man.
4. The wind blew steadily all night long, and when the sun's first rays shone weakly over the mountains, Caleb went out to quickly repair the storm's damage.
5. The old car shudders badly in high gear, but if you treat it nicely it'll get you where you want to go.
6. He wrote so illegibly that his teacher could barely make out the words.
7. I can hardly hear you!
8. His secret to success in life is to work hard, play often, and contribute as much as he can to whatever he does.
9. The writings of Voltaire inspired him, not so much esthetically as politically.
10. The right-wing faction insisted vociferously that their course of action was the only one that could be called morally correct.

✎ 16: Adjectives and Adverbs

Find the adjective/adverb errors and correct them.

DIAGNOSTICS

As they descended the walkway, the sights and sounds of the Moroccan city assailed their senses. They both walked slower and slower, as the crowd surged around them and the other passengers, almost impeding all movement. Men in bur-nooses, small boys peddling their cousin's hotel, women selling jewelry (probably stolen jewelry, she thought), they all covered the stone pier. Elbowing their way through the mass of people as quick as they could, Elsa and Robert finally stepped onto the mainland. Elsa felt unsettled, as if she'd been plunked down on a different planet. Haughty-looking camels waited, their halters held by disinterested-looking men. From somewhere nearby, coffee smelled strongly on the morning air. A wave of nausea came over Elsa, striking her unexpected, without warn-ing. But even as she fought it, she knew that here in Tangiers she would find what she'd set out to find. Life was treating her good.

✎ 17: Prepositions

Underline all prepositions.

1. Over the river and through the woods, to Grandmother's house we go.
2. One marmot scrambled over the log and one went around it.
3. Hold it under the running water for a while.
4. In a minute you'll see the horses come around the bend.
5. Behind the peeling bars of the cage, the lion paced back and forth, up and down the short concrete path.
6. To the right, marble columns formed a massive white wall, pulling the eyes toward the horizon.
7. Go across the street to the Hadleys' and see if they're home yet.
8. The band played "Underneath the Mango Tree" as we danced to the hypnotic island rhythms.
9. His signature was on the document, but he insisted that he'd signed it under duress.
10. Within the confines of the village, people were hurrying about, quiet and intent on their preparations; outside its walls, trees were bending to the ground, warning of the great storm that was on its way.

✎ 18: Conjunctions

Underline all conjunctions.

1. It was pouring, but they went out anyway.

2. In the afternoon, they had tea and crumpets.

3. He was laid off because he was always late to work.

4. We'll be able to afford to buy the house if the bank lends us $10,000.

5. Neither the President nor the First Lady saw the helicopter arrive.

6. When interest rates went down, they refinanced their house.

7. The actors bowed over and over while the audience applauded and cheered.

8. A mixture of milk, sugar and butter (or margarine) will make fudge, if the temperature is right; however, it must be stirred continuously while it cooks.

9. They changed the format when they raised their rates.

10. They sang along with the crowd, although they didn't know all the words.

✎ 19: Roots

Underline the root of each word and give its meaning.

1. inscription
2. teleportation
3. incredible
4. swimmer
5. input

6. biologist
7. fortunately
8. gradual
9. invisible
10. communication

✎ 20: Prefixes

Underline the prefix in each word and give its meaning.

1. indescribable
2. pronoun

6. deportation
7. exporting

3. reject
4. antipathy
5. corrupt

8. regression
9. inimitable
10. omniscient

✎ 21: Suffixes

Underline the suffix in each word and give its meaning.

1. interruption
2. careless
3. intrepidly
4. rapidity
5. uniqueness

6. rapacious
7. phonology
8. government
9. scientist
10. teacher

✎ 22: Roots and Affixes

Separate these words into their roots and affixes, then given the meaning of all of the parts, separately and together.

1. contact _____
2. adjunct _____
3. punitive _____
4. contraceptive _____
5. extraction _____

6. arborist _____
7. impenetrable _____
8. expulsion _____
9. ejection _____
10. synchronize _____

✎ 23: Word Families

Change the following words to supply the part of speech indicated.

1. colonial ⇒ N_____
2. routine ⇒ Adv _____
3. fright ⇒ V _____
4. heavy ⇒ Adv _____
5. imagine ⇒ N _____

6. flower ⇒ Adj _____
7. rage ⇒ V _____
8. fright ⇒ Adv _____
9. unique ⇒ Adv _____
10. circle ⇒ Adj _____

✎ 24: Parts of Speech

Indicate all parts speech for the following words.

1. separate _____
6. jerky _____

2. contact _____   7. fan _____

3. fine _____   8. proceeding _____

4. bend _____   9. rate _____

5. wound _____   10 brief _____

✎ 25: Verbs

Underline each verb, and indicate whether it's a true verb (T) or a copula (C). If it's a true verb, indicate whether it's active (A) or passive (P).

1. He sat writing, oblivious to the crowd that streamed past his bench.

2. In early fall, the diseased trees will be marked for the federal loggers.

3. The tide rose so quickly that they barely had time to scramble off the rocks and regain the shore.

4. Smoke rising from the campfire gave off a rich odor that permeated the woods.

5. By the end of the century, this corporation will have been completely taken over by government agencies.

6. Unsure where she was or how she'd gotten there, the young woman looked completely befuddled.

7. I'm sorry, but that just doesn't seem right.

8. What's for dinner? It smells wonderful!

9. I don't think these are my size, but they feel as if they fit me.

10. By the time the last nail had been pounded in, Kazimir's arm was sore from the effort.

✎ 26: Verbs

Underline infinitives once and gerunds twice.

1. To be or not to be, that is the question.

2. The duckling went slipping and sliding down the embankment into the water.

3. The goal of the starship was to go where no one had gone before.

4. The Agency had fully intended to include that point on their agenda, but because of procrastinating on the part of their secretary, it never got to the printer.

5. In terms of health, it's important to have a positive attitude and to get sufficient vigorous exercise; dieting doesn't do a bit of good.

6. If you forget to turn out the pilot light before you leave on vacation, the resulting explosion or fire could very well mark the ending of an otherwise wonderful trip.

7. The committee spoke to the administration to gain assurance that funding would be provided for additional staffing.

8. I didn't want to request any further instructions until I'd finished carrying out the previous ones.

9. Seeing is believing, they say, but I prefer to think that some of us can still act on faith.

10. She didn't have any trouble sightreading or accompanying someone on the piano, but performing solo in front of an audience was what she'd never been able to master.

✎ 27: Verbs

Label all auxiliary verbs and main verbs.

1. Have you seen "Gone with the Wind?"

2. As far as I know, my sister and her husband have never been to Lake Tahoe.

3. If you've never skied in the Alps, you haven't lived!

4. Carmello hasn't seen the new book yet, but I'm sure he'll be as pleased as if he'd written it himself.

5. Are they putting on the new roof today, or are they coming back tomorrow?

6. My parents don't know everything, but the older I get, the more impressed I am with how much they do know.

7. My brother is planning on applying to Stanford, but he's having trouble getting all the necessary applications.

8. Mr. Tran said that if you haven't finished going over his preliminary notes yet, you should wait until next week; by then he'll have finished transcribing them all.

9. You can bet your bottom dollar that if you haven't heard from them by now, they've probably run into trouble and have changed their minds about coming to work for you at all.

10. Czeslaw Milosz is a very famous writer who's won a Nobel Prize, but many people in the United States don't know him.

✎ 28: Verbs

Name the tense and mood of each verb.

1. An emu is a large, flightless bird indigenous to Australia.

2. I've never been to Australia, though, so I've never seen one in the wild.

3. Will doing crossword puzzles help increase my vocabulary?

4. I came, I saw, I conquered.

5. Go see what Michiko's doing, please.

6. The driving rain had already abated when they finished putting up the storm windows.

7. I would never have done it that way.

8. Each of these diagnostic exercises will help you determine whether you've understood the information in each section.

9. If only he were a little more understanding!

10. Have you ever seen anything so ridiculous?

✎ 29: Verbs

Underline all modals.

1. The plans must be ready by tomorrow.

2. You should rest for a few hours before tonight's performance.

3. If they don't check that company out first, they could wind up regretting having bought that stock.

4. You can stand in four states at one time in Four Corners, in the American southwest.

5. I read in the paper that they might cancel this year's Fourth of July fireworks.

6. If I were you, I wouldn't do that.

7. The government should spend more money on education and less on prisons.

8. Don't you think you ought to think about that some more?

9. I guess they can't come; they would have called by now if they were coming.

10. If greed goes unchecked, the rain-forests of the world might disappear during the next century.

✎ 30: Verbs

Underline each verb, and write T for Transitive and I for Intransitive.

1. The horses turned round and round as calliope music blared from the center of the carousel.

2. The breathless crowd stared, transfixed, while the acrobats executed one amazing flip after another.

3. He rinsed the plates and cups, filled the dishwasher and then shook out the crumb-covered tablecloth.

4. Stock prices have fallen, but if we survive this temporary setback without panicking, they'll surely rise again.

5. The radio played on and on to an empty bedroom, as Jeanette lingered in the bubble-bath, dreaming of Tahiti and the vacation of a lifetime that would start the next morning.

6. The hiring committee will meet tomorrow morning and go over all the applications together.

7. The violinists placed their bows on their instruments, and a hush swept across the audience.

8. Fortunately, Joshua had thought to bring a pocket-knife, and in no time at all he cut the vines that had ensnared Felipe's leg.

9. Her dive cut the water like a knife, and as soon as she disappeared beneath the surface, four dolphins sped to her side and began swimming alongside her.

10. Instead of finishing his homework, Alex procrastinated and made excuses, saying he'd already finished it and he really didn't have to do it anyway, and the teacher really only wanted the girls to do the homework, and they had the next day off anyway so he didn't have to hand it in for another three days.

✎ 31: Parts of Speech

Identify the underlined words.

The <u>airplane</u> <u>rose</u> sharply, climbing <u>to</u> an altitude of 30,000 feet. Below <u>the</u> wing, <u>she</u> could see the cities of <u>Sacramento</u> <u>and</u> West Sacramento stretching across the <u>flat</u> plains <u>along</u> <u>its</u> two rivers, the Sacramento and the American. To the north, rice fields <u>glistened</u> <u>brightly</u> in the sun. <u>They</u> looked like huge squares <u>and</u> rectangles of ice, or <u>gigantic</u> mirrors. <u>Dipping</u> <u>sharply</u> to the right, the plane banked and turned, and <u>finally</u>, covering the brilliant sun with a wing, <u>it</u> <u>straightened</u> and headed like an arrow toward the <u>snow-capped</u> Sierra Nevada, <u>the</u> towering <u>mountains</u> to the east.

The Next Step:

COMBINING
THE
INGREDIENTS

Now you've got all the ingredients down off your shelf and you've named them all. What next?

Before you proceed further, be sure you're completely familiar with what everything's called and with what it does (Parts I and II). Do all the Diagnostics for both Parts. If you score above 80% correct on those, you can go on to Part III; but for even more proficiency, do the Practices, too. The better you know the basic stuff, the easier it'll be to grab something off the shelf when your mixture starts to boil over!

PART III

Mixing the Dough and Slicing the Apples

The next thing you, the chef, have to master in your kitchen is how to put the ingredients together (did you spot the separable phrasal verb there? – "put ... together"). Not all together right away; before you put your pie in the oven, you have to first prepare the crust and then the apples. When you're sure they're each right, then – and only then – you put them together. Before your dumplings go in the stew, both the dumplings and the stew have to be mixed correctly, separately.

To create a main dish of sentences, paragraphs, essays, letters, reports, etc., you need to understand phrases and clauses. So let's lay them out on your counter one by one and see how they're made and what they do.

✧ ✧ ✧

♦ PHRASE

A phrase is a group of words that has no subject-verb combination. (Compare with Clause, next section.) The following is a noun:

man

But add another word to it and it becomes a phrase:

a man

(art.) (noun)

Now add another, or maybe two:

a tall, handsome man
(art.)(adj)   (adj)   (noun)

This is a phrase, because more than one word is used to express the thought. The following are all phrases :

the blue book
with a shake of its tail
hardly blinking an eye
on the table
holding the door open with one foot

There are many different types of phrases. Basically, a phrase is classified according to the job it does: noun phrase, adjective phrase, adverbial phrase, etc. There are probably as many types of phrases as there are parts of speech ... but you don't need to worry about memorizing all the types. Just remember: a phrase is a group of words. "Group" means that the words belong together. Consider this:

✗ with a long, loud

What's wrong with that phrase? Of course: there's at least one word missing (the adjectives "long" and "loud" need a noun with them to make sense). Or this:

✗ on the floor next to

Same thing: this is a phrase and a half. "On the floor" stands by itself – a prepositional phrase – but the second prepositional phrase is incomplete without its noun.

Let's look at some of the different ways phrases can work in a sentence. First, here are some noun phrases:

a loving glance
(noun)
their oversized, enthusiastic hound
(noun)
an old, battered sofa
(noun)

The main word, what the speaker/writer is talking about, is a noun, so it's called a noun phrase.

Now some verb phrases:

The kids were <u>screaming and shouting and hopping up and down.</u>
The boat <u>rolled and pitched.</u>

If a phrase modifies a noun, it's an **adjectival phrase:**
  the boy <u>with the big, brown eyes</u>
> (this adjectival phrase is also a prepositional phrase, since it's introduced by a preposition)

And if a phrase modifies a verb, it's an **adverbial phrase.**
He ran quickly <u>enough to win the race.</u>
> (How quickly did he run? Only an adverb modifies another adverb.)

She sang **with an unequalled purity of voice.**
> (this prepositional phrase modifies "sang")

Of course, in the real world it's not so simple! One sentence can have many phrases. Let's look at some complete sentences that use phrases:

<u>The shiny, weird-looking white car</u> <u>in the garage</u> is the one that <u>my father</u> drove <u>to win the race.</u>
> Noun Phrase: The shiney, weird-looking white car ...
> Prep. Phrase: ... in the garage
> Noun Phrase: ... my father ...
> Adverbial Infinitive Phrase: ... to win the race. (modifying "used:" Why did he use it?)

<u>The biggest, most expensive painting</u> <u>was stolen</u> <u>from the collection.</u>
> Noun Phrase: The biggest, most expensive painting ...
> Verb Phrase: ... was stolen ...
> Prep. Phrase: ... from the collection.

If you run <u>like the dickens,</u> you might get there <u>soon enough to buy a ticket.</u>
> Adverbial Phrase: ... like the dickens ... (how fast do you run?_)
> Adv. Phrase: ... soon enough ... (how soon do you get there?)
> Adverbial Infinitive Phrase: ... to buy a ticket.
>   (modifying "soon enough")

Note: If you speak another language, don't be confused by the word "phrase." In many languages, the equivalent word "phrase" or "frase" means "sentence." In English, though, it only means a group of words. A phrase is NOT a sentence.

 How to identify a phrase: Ask yourself: Does this group of words have a subject- verb combination? If **not,** it's a **phrase.** If it does, it's a ...

♦ CLAUSE

A group of words that has a subject and verb (or predicate). First, let's define our terms:

Subject is the person or thing that's doing the action of the verb.

Verb (see Part II, Verb).

Predicate is the verb and whatever elements complete it (verb and its complement).

<u>Cedars</u> <u>grow</u> at high elevations
(Subj. noun) (V)

<u>Tall, fragrant cedar trees</u> <u>grow at high elevations</u>
(Subj. noun phrase) (Pred.)

<u>His mentor</u> <u>was a tall, sparse man with a moustache.</u>
(Subj.) (Pred.)

Look at the difference between a phrase and a clause. They are both groups of words, but only a clause has both a subject and verb. A phrase can have a verb (grow at high elevations), but there's no subject to go with it. Or it can have a noun that looks like a subject (Tall, fragrant cedar trees), but there's no accompanying verb. But put those two elements (phrases) together and you have a clause. Let's look at a few :

<u>we're studying</u> grammar
(subj) (verb)

<u>the accident</u> <u>was</u> on the news last night
(subj) (verb)

Either the subject or the verb of any clause can be composed of more than one element. For example, consider the following clause:

<u>Mom and Dad</u> <u>went</u> to the movies...
(subj) (verb)

The subject in this clause is composed of two nouns; Mom and Dad (a compound subject; compound = composed of more than one element). But they have a simple (only one) verb, so this is **one clause**. Conversely:

<u>they</u> <u>ate</u> dinner and <u>went</u> to a movie ...
(subj) (verb) (verb)

The simple subject of this clause, 'they', has two verbs: **ate** and **went** (a compound verb). So it's one clause.

If you were to draw a diagram of the two previous clauses, they might look like this :

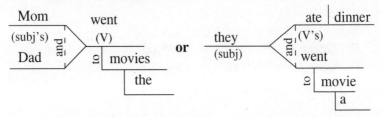

If there is only one Subject-Verb combination, even if both the subject and verb are compound, it is one clause. In this case, the conjunction (and, or...) is between the elements of either the subject or the verb (like in the two examples above). If the conjunction is placed after the whole clause, then you're dealing with a compound or complex sentence, which is covered in Part IV, Sentences.

NOTE: If a single clause stands alone and expresses a complete thought, it is called a **simple sentence** (see Part IV, Sentence). A sentence can have more than one clause.

Let's sum up this section on clauses with a little visual scheme of their construction:

2 PARTS OF A CLAUSE:	WHAT EACH PART IS COMPOSED OF:
1. Subject	Noun, pronoun or noun phrase
2. Predicate	Verb (or verb phrase) and its complements*, if any

*The Complement of a verb consists of any combination of the following:

VERB +   Direct Object (He read <u>the book</u>)
           Indirect Object (I gave <u>him</u> the book)
           Predicate Noun/s (She was <u>the pilot</u>)
           Predicate Adjective/s (The ocean was <u>calm</u>)

Examples (the predicates are in **bold** type):
The painter **painted the wrong color on the wall**.
         (V.)   (D. O.)   (Prep. Phr.)

The secretary **gave** **me** **the application form.**
          (V.) (I.O.)   (D. O.)

Dr. Nowicki **was my biology teacher.**
          (Cop. V.)   (Pred. Nom.)

The speaker, Mrs. Nguyen, **looked tiny and frail.**
              (Cop. V.) (Pred. Adj.'s)

How to identify complements:

1. A **Direct Object** answers the question "Whom?" or "What?" about the verb.

2. An **Indirect Object** answers the question "To what?" or "To whom?" about the verb.

3. The **Object of a Preposition** is the noun that follows a preposition in a prepositional phrase.

4. **Predicate Nominative** or **Adjective** completes the equation: Subject = _____ (the equal sign being a copulative verb).

Like phrases, clauses can also take on the job of different parts of speech. A clause can act like a noun, an adjective or an adverb. Let's see how.

♦ **1. Noun Clauses**

A clause that acts like a noun can have either of the jobs of a noun: subject or object. They are part of a larger clause (since that's the job of a subject or object).

That they finish on time was the single most important factor.
    (subj.)

She asked when we would arrive.
          (Dir. Obj.)

♦ **2. Adjective Clauses**

... modify nouns and pronouns in another clause.

The performance, which began late, was a big hit.

The performer was a local boy who had become famous.

The auditorium where they performed was too small.

Adjective clauses usually begin with the relative pronouns **who, whom, that** or **which.** They can also begin with **when, where** or **why.**

♦ **3. Adverb Clauses**

... modify verbs, adjectives or adverbs. They begin with a conjunction, and like adverbs, they usually tell why, when, where, how, or how much.

The Starship would go where no ship had gone before.

She made the doll look as pretty as she could.

They ran as quickly as they could with their heavy boots.

♦ **4. Independent Clauses**

... stand on their own, grammatically. Their meaning is clear without any other clause needed for further clarification.

♦ **5. Dependent Clauses**

... can't stand on their own. They depend on another clause for their meaning. For example, consider the following sentence:

I stopped for milk on the way home, *but* the store was closed.

If you remove the conjunction **but**, either of the clauses in that sentence can be a sentence on its own:

● I stopped for milk on the way home.
● The store was closed.

These clauses are **independent**. Now try this:

● The home they bought last year has a lovely, secluded garden.

Let's separate that into its two component clauses:

● The home has a lovely, secluded garden
● (that) they bought last year

The second clause **cannot** stand by itself. With or without its relative word, it needs the other clause to make its meaning clear (you can't say "they bought last year," since "bought" requires an object). This second clause is a **dependent** clause.

We'll see more about that when we talk about Sentences, in the next section ....

(But don't forget to do all the Diagnostics for this Section first.)

DIAGNOSTICS

PART III

✎ 32: Phrases and Clauses

Write P before each Phrase and C before each clause.

_____ 1. after mixing the ingredients
_____ 2. the car didn't come to a complete stop
_____ 3. if you've never swum in the ocean
_____ 4. having come to a quick conclusion
_____ 5. the brown suitcase and its matching duffel bag
_____ 6. imitation is the sincerest form of flattery
_____ 7. having gone through it himself, he had a good idea what it was like
_____ 8. night fell
_____ 9. night fall
_____ 10. rolling over and over in the soft sand

✎ 33: Phrases and Clauses

Underline all phrases and indicate their type (preposition, noun, adjective, adverb, gerund ...). Remember: some phrases can fit more than one category.

1. She sent her impudent son to his room without his supper.
2. The little boy shouted and waved, but his voice was inaudible over the roar of the surf.
3. I just did it for a joke.
4. The two tomcats faced each other, hissing and snarling.
5. Laughing and crying at the same time, the two old friends fell into each other's arms,
6. The bonfire only burned for a few minutes.
7. Two hundred soldiers marched off to battle, following the sound of the bagpiper.
8. After the movie, everybody went to the little cafe on the square and had coffee with their dessert.
9. Seated on a large, flat rock, the young girl dangled her bare feet in the icy water.

10. The deer paused at the top of the ravine, unsure about their footing and anxious about the two strange, two--footed creatures that faced them from the other side.

✎ 34: Phrases and Clauses

Identify each of the underlined portions of the following passage as a Phrase or Clause. If it's a phrase, indicate its type.

As <u>the last two people</u> took their seats, a hush fell <u>over the expectant audience</u>. <u>Someone coughed</u>. When the conductor raised her baton, it was as if <u>the whole audience released the collective breath</u> they'd been holding. <u>Violins and violas</u> began suddenly, followed by the basses. The timpani <u>crashed and rumbled,</u> and without warning, <u>out of nowhere</u>, the eerie vibration of a gong rang out over the music. The sound of the strings diminished until they were <u>barely audible</u>. Trombones and trumpets took up the melody <u>after that</u>, playing with a vigor and volume that made <u>the listeners' seats</u> vibrate.

✎ 35: Phrases and Clauses

Underline all <u>Independent Clauses</u> once and <u>Dependent Clauses</u> twice.

1. That's the road that we should've taken.
2. I need the unbrella that's in the closet.
3. The road that's the straightest isn't always the best.
4. This place has the best food I've ever tasted!
5. Did you see the sign that said there was a detour?
6. They asked for our passports, which we didn't have with us.
7. The boy who was asleep in the back seat missed all the excitement.
8. John Sutter, who owned the mill where gold was discovered in California, died a poor man.
9. In order to maximize profits, we shall have to abandon the project we began last quarter.
10. The cows that are in the lower pasture will soon be moving up to higher ground that's still snow-covered.

PUTTING THE PIE TOGETHER

You've prepared the apple mixture and the dough separately; now it's time to mix all those ingredients together and put the whole thing in the oven to become something people will enjoy. Some chefs make it plain and simple; some create elaborate lattice-work shells or sprinkle cinnamon or sugar or other fancy stuff on top; this is where it gets creative!

Sentences

A sentence is a group of words that expresses a complete thought, with at least one subject and predicate.

That sounds very much like the definition of a clause, but with this difference: a sentence expresses a complete thought. If the sentence has only one clause, it's called a simple sentence.

Here are a few clauses. Some can be sentences, some can't:

1. it's raining
2. when I went to the bank
3. before the doors close
4. putting clauses together is the last step in creating sentences
5. some people say
6. which equals a multiple of ten
7. the Chairman of the Board will answer questions after the meeting
8. after the meeting convenes next Tuesday
9. that we bought with the money from the lottery
10. we bought a new home with the money from the lottery

Can you tell which ones are incomplete? (2, 3, 5, 6, 8 and 9) What makes them incomplete?

Words like *when, before, after,* are called **subordinating conjunctions** (con-joining two clauses). They signal the fact that the clause they introduce is **subordinate**, or incomplete without another to give it meaning. (Notice the root and affixes: sub = less, lower than; ordin = order; -ate = adjective; thus, subordinate means less in importance or substance, lower in the order of importance.)

If you say, for example, "When I went to the bank," everyone will be listening for the rest of the information. What happened when you went to the bank? The subordinate information, "when I went to the bank," doesn't stand on its own. What happened will be the other, independent, clause.

Clauses #1, 4, 7 and 10 can be complete sentences by themselves, by adding a capital letter and punctuation, or they can each be part of a compound or complex sentence (made of two or more clauses), like this:

It's raining, and I forgot my umbrella. (compound)

The Chairman of the Board will answer questions after the meeting, which will take place on Friday at noon. (complex)

 A clause that can stand on its own is called **independent.** One that requires further information for meaning is **dependent.**

Now, let's modify slightly a definition that bears repeating:

 A sentence is a group of words that expresses a complete thought, and includes at least one clause.

✧ ✧ ✧

Sentence Construction

There are four types of sentence construction:

1. Simple
2. Compound
3. Complex
4. Compound-complex

♦ 1. Simple Sentence

A simple sentence consists of one independent clause. See #1, 4, 7 and 10, previously. Length has nothing to do with it. A simple sentence can be long or short.

It seldom rains in the desert.

The wheat, waving and dancing in the summer breeze, was like a vast, rolling sea of gold.

♦ 2. Compound Sentence

A compound sentence has two or more independent clauses, usually joined by a conjunction or by punctuation.

Jacques speaks French   and   Ali speaks Farsi
‾‾‾‾‾‾‾‾‾‾‾‾‾‾‾‾‾‾‾   (conj) ‾‾‾‾‾‾‾‾‾‾‾‾‾‾‾
        (clause)   (clause)

It started to snow when they left the house.
(clause)   (conj)   (clause)

Pawns moves straight, rooks move straight, but
(clause)   (clause)

knights move in a L shape
(clause)

Length has nothing to do with it;
(clause)

a simple sentence can be long or short
(clause)

The conjunction that joins two equal (coordinate) clauses is called a **coordinate conjunction.** (Co- = with, together, and ordinate- = order; in other words, conjoining clauses of the same order or type.)

♦ 3. Complex Sentence

A complex sentence has at least one independent clause and at least one dependent clause.

(The clauses in italics are the dependent clauses, they depend on the main clauses for their meaning.)

The coat *that I bought yesterday* is on sale today.
We're reading books *that we should've read before.*

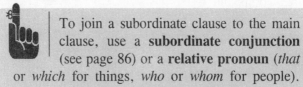

To join a subordinate clause to the main clause, use a **subordinate conjunction** (see page 86) or a **relative pronoun** (*that* or *which* for things, *who* or *whom* for people).

♦ 4. Compound-complex Sentence

In the following sentence, there are two independent clauses and one dependent; this is the fourth type of sentence, compound-complex, a combination of the two previous types.

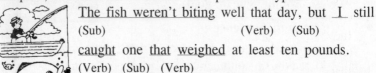

The fish weren't biting well that day, but I still
(Sub)   (Verb)   (Sub)

caught one that weighed at least ten pounds.
(Verb) (Sub) (Verb)

Note: In this sentence, the relative word, "that," is the **subject** of the verb "weighed." That makes it a **relative pronoun,** not a conjunction ("that" takes the place of "one," meaning fish). In the two complex sentences, above, the **relative pronouns** "that" act as the **objects** of the verbs.

Now let's take apart a sentence of each type to see how it's really put together. Let's start with:

Simple Sentence
They climbed a mountain.
(pro/sub)   (verb)   (noun/obj)
(predicate)

Now let's make it a compound predicate, but with still only one subject:

Simple Sentence with Compound Predicate
They went backpacking, and climbed a mountain.
(pro/subj)   (predicate)   (conj)   (predicate)

Let's add a second independent clause:

Compound Sentence
We stayed at the camp, but they climbed a mountain.
(subj)   (predicate)   (coord. (subj)   (predicate) conj.)

Now let's add subordinate information (a dependent clause).

Complex Sentence
They climbed a mountain that they'd never climbed.
(subj)   (predicate)   (rel pro) (subj)   (predicate)

And finally, longer still:

Compound Complex Sentence
We stayed at the camp, but
(subj)   (predicate)   (conj)
they climbed a mountain
(subj)   (predicate)
that they'd never climbed before.
(rel pro) (subj)   (predicate)
(dependent cluase)

♦ Mood

What kind of mood does grammar put you in?

No. we're not talking about that kind. **Mood** indicates the attitude of the writer or speaker toward what he's writing or saying. It's a variation of the word *mode* and comes from the Latin word *modus,* meaning manner or tune/tone (what tone does the sentence set?). There are three main grammatical moods:

1. Indicative - a statement of fact

> It's raining outside.

The following are functions of the Indicative mood:

● **Declarative** - a statement

> I believe it's raining.

● **Interrogative** - a question

> Is it raining?

> This is considered indicative, since every question can be converted back into its declarative form.

> What does that mean? ⇒ That means what (+ question)

> Does he speak French? ⇒ He speaks French (+ question)

● **Exclamatory** - an exclamation

> This is so easy!

2. Imperative - a command

> Sit down and read this.

Notice that the subject in an imperative sentence isn't expressed. Both the speaker and the listener (or the reader and writer) know who they mean. so it goes without saying. This is called an **understood subject**, or "you, understood". In a diagram, this is usually represented by parentheses:

Read this article ⇒ (You) | read | article
this

3. Subjunctive - expresses wishes or conditions that are contrary to fact. request. or demands (see also Part II. Verbs, p. 46). Usually used in dependent clauses (p. 82):

> If this were as difficult as you thought, this book would be longer. (it isn't that difficult; this statement is contrary to fact)

> They've requested that she be there before the meeting starts.

♦ Normal Word Order

> Word order this the normal isn't.
> Isn't this order word the normal.
> Order word normal the isn't this.

What's wrong with the above three sentences? Obviously, the words are out of order. But what's the correct order, and how much variation can that order stand?

In English, the normal word order for a sentence is **S-V-O** (Subject - Verb - Object). If there's no object, then just **S-V** (or Pred.)

The dog bit the mailman.
S   V   O

But if you change the order, it's difficult to tell who did what to whom:

Bit the mailman the dog.   The dog the mailman bit.
V   S?/O?   S?/O?   S?/O?   S?/O?   V

If they're out of order, we have no way of knowing the relationships between the words. Other languages show those relationships by endings, or changes in spelling, or other types of modulation. In English, we have only the sentence structure to give order to our words.

Some words are movable. Adverbs, for example, can go just about anywhere, depending on the emphasis, for example:

Eventually, they ran out of money.
They ran out of money *eventually*.

Or:

Adverbs can easily be moved to a different place in the sentence.

Adverbs can be moved *easily* to a different place in the sentence.

Adverbs can be moved to a different place in the sentence *easily*.

But in terms of general sentence structure, the formula to remember is: **S-V-O.**

Before studying the schematic table below, **Parts of a Sentence**, let's refresh our memories:

a **PHRASE** is a group of words. (no subject/verb combination)

a **CLAUSE** is a group of words that has a subject and verb/predicate

a **SENTENCE** is a group of words that expresses a complete thought, containing at least one cluase.

Now we're ready to sum up:

♦ **A SCHEMATIC TABLE - Parts of a Sentence**

1. Simple Sentence		
SUBJECT	+	PREDICATE
Art/Adj. + Noun(s) Noun Phrase(s)		verb(s) (+ Adverbial/s) (+ Complement/s)
2. Compound Sentence		
IND. CLAUSE (Subject + Predicate)	+ CONJUNCTION+ (or punctuation)	IND. CLAUSE, etc. (Subject + Predicate)
3. Complex Sentence **Combination of**		
INDEPENDENT CLAUSE	+ RELATIVE WORD conjunction(s) or pronoun(s) or punctuation	+ DEPENDENT CLAUSE(S)
4. Compound-Complex Sentence		
Same as 3, Complex Sentence, but with more than one independent clause.		

DIAGNOSTICS

PART IV

✎ 36. Sentences

Change each sentence to a statement (declarative), and indicate the subject and verb. (Some words may need to be changed or deleted)

1. Don't you have any money?

2. Are you going to the party on Friday?

3. Hasn't that package arrived yet?

4. Are they going to be finished by tomorrow, or shall I come back next week?

5. Should I have called sooner?

6. Is freedom of speech one of the most important rights we have?

7. If you're going to be late, shouldn't you call and let them know?

8. Would they have gone anyway, even if they had known?

9. Which museum is that painting in?

10. Do you believe in extra-terrestrial life?

✎ 37. Sentences

Write **S** for simple, **C** for compound, **Cx** for complex or **C-Cx** for a compound-complex sentence.

_____ 1. Cherries will be in season from now until the end of the month.

_____ 2. While they were camping at Sequoia National Park, someone there was bitten by a bear.

_____ 3. Despite their high prices, fur coats never seem to go out of fashion.

____ 4. Speak now, or forever hold your peace.

____ 5. Which do you prefer, orange or grape?

____ 6. I'll have the one you just finished mixing.

____ 7. If you mix the crimson with a little light yellow, you'll get a lovely color that'll bring out the highlights of the flowers in the landscape.

8. He sat on the park bench writing postcards, lost in memories of their good times together.

9. She couldn't get the cap off the brake fluid reservoir, although she tried all the tools in the garage.

10. Over and over, the two bear cubs tumbled down the embankment, snarling and clawing and biting at each other and having the time of their lives.

✎ 38: Sentences

Write **I** for indicative, **Imp** for imperative or **S** for subjunctive.

____ 1. When travelling in the desert, it's always advisable to carry lots of water.

____ 2. Open the hood and check the oil.

____ 3. When was the last time you went to an amusement park?

____ 4. It's important that you do your best at the interview.

____ 5. There's a fire in the attic!

____ 6. Please come in and have a seat.

____ 7. The Management requires that you keep accurate records and submit all requests at least one week in advance.

____ 8. Dad attached a joystick to the computer, so now we can play all kinds of neat games.

_____ 9. I wish he were a millionaire.

_____ 10. When the booth is empty, step inside, place your card in the holder, and register your vote by using the little marker pin on the chain to the right.

✎ 39: Sentences

In the following passage, Indicate the type of each sentence (S for simple, Cd for compound. Cx for complex, and Cd-Cx for compound-complex), and its mood (I for Indicative, Imp for Imperative, or Sub for subjunctive).

1) Johann August Sutter, the founder of the city of Sacramento, came to California in a roundabout way. 2) To escape debt. he left his native Switzerland and traveled to the midwest of the United States. 3) From there, he made the trek to the north-west, but he only stayed there a short while. 4) Can you guess where he went next? 5) He sailed to Hawaii, which fascinated him with its lush mountains, natural beauty and impressive people. 6) The king there was equally fascinated by Sutter, so when this strange adventurer from across the sea left the islands, the king gave him a cadre of his strongest warriors to accompany him to the mainland. 7) Once there, Sutter got a land grant from the Governor of what was then part of Mexico, and built his famous mill in a spot which would later yield that yellow metal that would draw people to California from all over the world. 8) It was imperative that he keep the discovery to himself. 9) However, his ex-partner, Sam Brannan, was soon broadcasting the news to all of San Francisco while he sold shovels, picks and other prospector's items from his wagon there. 10) And after the frenzy of the Gold Rush, John Sutter died a poor man.

DIAGNOSTICS

1. ____ / ____   6. ____ / ____
2. ____ / ____   7. ____ / ____
3. ____ / ____   8. ____ / ____
4. ____ / ____   9. ____ / ____
5. ____ / ____   10. ____ / ____

The Final Steps:

SETTING A
BEAUTIFUL TABLE

If you wanted you could take everything you've learned so far and put it together any way you wanted theoretically anyone would understand you since the words are all their in the write order order is everything right well no in language like in many things in life attention to detail makes all the difference.

Can you read that beginning paragraph? Of course; but it takes some work. And generally speaking, unless it's proud parents trying to decipher their child's first writings, people won't take the time or expend the effort to decipher your writing - or your speech - if the details are missing or wrong.

The next two Parts of this book deal with those details, called punctuation and spelling. (For the corrected version of the paragraph above, see "Answers to Diagnostics-Punctuation," but first, try to correct it yourself)

Seasoning the Ingredients or Punctuation

Punctuation is the way to get from Point A to Point B in English. It's the road map, the sign-posts that tell you where to stop, where to pause, where to put emphasis. It can make a sentence understandable or turn it into gibberish. It's the numbering of the steps in the recipe.

It's like making soup. If you boil just the water for hours, then add the other ingredients and serve, your soup is going to taste like water. No one will know it's soup. You must follow the steps, in the right order, and everyone else must be able to tell, by the taste, that you did. If you add the carrots to the soup but don't pause in the process to give them time to soften, it won't be right. The soup may taste delicious, but what we'll remember is the work our teeth had to do to eat it. Commas tell us when to pause; periods tell us when to stop. Exchange a question mark or exclamation point for a period and see the difference it makes.

Every element of punctuation has an essential job in guiding the reader along the path laid by our words. Punctuation used wrongly can send the reader the wrong message. Used well, it can bring life to your words and touch the reader. It can spice up your basic recipe, making it memorable for those who consume your words. It's like eggs - pretty bland stuff, all alone. But a souffle, created and served by a world-class chef, can be an unforgettable experience!

Let's take a look at the basic elements of punctuation and how they work.

✧ ✧ ✧

♦ **1. Period**

Used at the end of a complete indicative sentence (a statement).

The use of the period is self-explanatory.

♦ 2. Exclamation point

Used after a sentence or interjection to indicate strong emotion.

> Hurry up! The hurricane's coming!
> Damn!
> I said, "Sit down!" (This is more than a simple quote; the speaker is putting emphasis on his words.)

♦ 3. Question mark

Used at the end of a question.

> Have you learned the use of the comma yet?
> How much is 10 to the 4th power?

♦ 4. Comma

1) Used within a sentence to indicate **a pause.**

That's a general rule-of-thumb. If you read what you write out loud, you can hear where the commas go. For example, Harry would be pretty upset if his buddies didn't get the punctuation right on these two sentences:

> "Shoot, Harry"
> "Shoot Harry!"

But let's enlarge on that definition: The comma is:

2) Used when listing similar items:

> She bought coffee, bread, sugar, milk and butter.
>
> They stole a valuable watch, a diamond necklace and several old paintings.
>
> The sculpture was pointed at the ends, round in the center and bright orange.

Some grammar books put a comma between the last two items on the list. before the word "and." However, you can also think of it this way:

> She bought coffee and bread and sugar and milk and butter.   ,   ,   ,

The commas replace all the conjunctions, serving the same purpose. If you keep the conjunction between the last two, you don't need anything else - unless the last two words form a unit without it.

For example, if the first sentence read like this: She bought coffee, milk, sugar, bread and butter: Sometimes the words "bread and butter" are used together as a chunk phrase, but they're not meant that way here; if you mean them separately, use the comma. Otherwise, the comma and the conjunction serve the same purpose, so to use both is redundant. Often, though, it's a question of style. As you develop your own, you can make your own choices.

3) Used between words that are out of their normal order.

Harrington, Thomas
I'd like tea, Darjeeling.

This one also covers that old rule they taught you in school, that says you must use a comma if you begin a sentence with an introductory phrase.

After the game, they went out for pizza.
Despite all his bragging, he finished in third place.

Think of it this way: The adverbial phrase (after the game) really modifies the verb (went). Normally, the adverb is placed after the verb. Since it's out of its normal order here (it's before the noun, not after the verb), you need a comma.

4) Used between words that belong to different categories.

Paris, France (city and country)
Arlington, Virginia (city and state)
September 23, 1951 (day and year)

You probably also learned in school that you use a comma after each part of an address. That's because of this rule of different categories. For example:

He works as an Instructor of English at American River College, 4700 College Oak Drive, Sacramento, California. (a string of nouns placed one next to the other; but each belonging to different categories: school, street address. city. state)

Did you say Portland, Maine or Portland, Oregon? (city state)

5) Used to separate non-essential, or nonrestrictive, information from the rest of the clause.

Walnuts, which my brother can't stand, are a major ingredient in the recipe. (The main statement here is that walnuts are a major ingredient; the fact that my brother can't stand them is non-essential to understanding the main clause)

Jan Paderewski, a famous Polish pianist, appeared in Carnegie Hall the year my father was born. (The main fact here is that Paderewski appeared in Carnegie Hall that year; the appositive, the fact that he was a famous Polish pianist, is nice to know but unnecessary to understand the main clause,)

 This applies to all non-restrictive Nouns in Apposition.

The Statue of Liberty, which stands in New York Harbor, was an inspiring symbol of freedom to the immigrants who crossed the Atlantic by boat. (The main clause tells us that the Statue was a symbol of freedom. The fact that it was in N.Y. Harbor is nice to know but not essential)

Non-essential information also includes all the rules you tried to learn in school about interjections, direct address, tag questions, etc. All of these things are elements that don't belong to any grammatical part of the sentence. They're non-essential. Consider the following (the italicized elements are not essential to the grammatical sentence):

My God, Waldbaum had gone up the mountain alone!

This is the only planet we have, *isn't it?*

Class, today we're going to have a speaker.

But don't use a comma if the appositive or other element is necessary to the meaning of the sentence/clause (restrictive). In the following sentences, the appositive is necessary to understand the speaker's meaning:

The class (that) I took last semester was cancelled. (Without the appositive, you don't know which class,)

The singer Perry Como was popular during the 1960s. (Without the appositive, you don't know which singer I'm talking about.)

But:

The singer, Perry Como, returned to the stage for several encores. (Here, both listener and speaker know which singer; but the speaker adds his name as additional - non-essential -information.)

● Comma Splice

It's easy to over-use a comma. It's a powerful tool, but like any tool, you must use it only when it's appropriate. You wouldn't use a jackhammer to drill a tiny hole in a cabinet, or a hammer to crack open your soft-boiled egg. Similarly, remember that a comma indicates a slight pause, a breath pause; it does not represent a full stop (only a period does that) or a change of topic. And if the pause represents a change of logic - a contradiction, for example, or contrast, or a slight shift in topic - the least you can expect to use is a semi-colon.

An overuse of any of these types is called a comma splice. Splice means to attach, and sometimes commas are used wrongly to attach elements that should be separated by something stronger. For example:

✗ When we went to Yellowstone, we saw lots of wildlife, we also saw tourists on every rock and path.

✔ When we went to Yellowstone, we saw lots of wildlife. We also saw tourists on every rock and path.

You can also fix a comma splice by joining the two clauses with punctuation or with a conjunction. For example:

✗ The funds can be allocated to Research, they can be used by Instructional Development.

✔ The funds can be allocated to Research, or they can be used by Instructional Development.

✗ When you paint with oils, the colors stay moist for hours, when you paint with acrylics, they dry out fast.

✔ When you paint with oils, the colors stay moist for hours; when you paint with acrylics, they dry out fast.

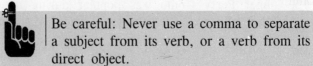

Be careful: Never use a comma to separate a subject from its verb, or a verb from its direct object.

✗ The long, colorful streamers, extended from one side of the room to the other.

✔ The long, colourful streamers extended from one side of
       (sub)   (verb)
the room to the other.

✗ St. Petersburg's celebrated museum contains, a wealth
of Russian art.

✔ St. Petersburg's celebrated museum contains a wealth
                                   (verb)   (dir.obj.)
of Russian art.

But: If some other element is inserted between the verb and its object, a comma may be necessary:

This museum *contains*, among other things,
                  (verb)
a reproduction of Rodin's sculpture, "The Thinker."
(dir. obj)

♦ 5. Semi-colon

Indicates a pause that's longer than a comma but not as complete as a period. Mostly used to link independent clauses and to separate items in a series; often shows contrast.

Sugar floats in iced tea; in hot coffee, it melts.

Today the painters will strip the existing paint; tomorrow they'll begin the new work.

A noise like the rumbling of a subway swept through the building; it was an earthquake.

City life can be exciting; life in the country, however, is easier on the nerves.

As a freshman, I dabbled in sports; as a sophomore, I ventured into the world of music by joining the orchestra; but as a senior, I found so many fields of endeavor to my liking that I couldn't decide which to try, and wound up doing nothing at all.

♦ 6. Colon

Used to introduce something.

You can think of a colon as a trumpet blast, the drum roll that leads us to expect clarification, or an example, or some further information. For example:

When you come to the exam, please bring the following : two pencils, some scratch paper, a calculator and a watch.

The names of wines, more than their taste, have always beckoned me to the exotic, far-away places where they were born; Bordeaux, Champagne, Chianti, Zinfandel, even Napa, Sonoma and Mendocino.

♦ 7. Quotation marks

Used around direct quotations (using someone else's exact words) and titles of short works.

> She said, "Tomorrow we'll have a quiz on punctuation."
> In Poe's famous poem, "The Raven," the bird in question says the same word over and over throughout the long story: "Nevermore."

Also used to signal a definition:

> In French, prix fixe means a "fixed price."

But not in a paraphrase of a definition:

> In French, a prix fixe meal on a menu means that you pay a certain preset price and nothing more.

Also used to indicate irony or unusual usage:

> Her first "classroom" was nothing more than a table and some chairs set up under the big oak tree.
> The "meat" of the essay is hidden among the multi-syllabic words and strange descriptions and almost frivolous side-trips that the author takes us on.

● Using Quotation Marks with other Punctuation

Periods and commas go inside the closing quotation mark.

> "Ask not what your country can do for you," said John Kennedy, "ask what you can do for your country."
> "I wouldn't do that if I were you," warned his partner.

As you can see in the above example, the period of the quoted remark becomes a comma when the quote ends before the sentence.

Other punctuation goes inside the quotation marks if they're part of the quotation, outside if they're not.

> Inside: The medic asked, "Are you all right?"
> Outside: How many of you know the words to "The Star-Spangled Banner"?

Inside: "Look out!" shouted one of the rescuers.

Outside: Not a single student had heard of "The Scarlet Letter"!

 Note: Never use quotation marks with an indirect quote. An indirect quote paraphrases someone else's words instead of using the exact words.

Indirect: They predicted that he would finish the race third.

Direct: "He's going to finish in third place," they predicted.

♦ 8. Apostrophe

Used in the following three ways:

1) Possessive

The possessive case shows ownership. The possessive is formed by adding **'s** to a word, unless it's a plural word that ends with **s.**

Mike**'s** cake/the chef**'s** hat/the children**'s** party
somebody**'s** car/Nguyen**'s** books

BUT: the Clarks' house/ten dollars' worth/students' desks

To make it a little clearer, think of it this way: The possessive is shown in speech by the sound of S/Z at the end of the word (Mike**'s**, children's). If the word itself already ends with a plural S/Z sound (the Clark**s**, ten dollar**s**), you don't need another one.

 When in doubt write the word, singular or plural, and add **'s**. Then, if you hear two S/Z sounds at the end, drop the last one:
the students'$\cancel{s}$ desks / two cents'$\cancel{s}$ worth

2) Contractions

Whenever a letter is dropped from a word or between words, this omission is shown by adding an apostrophe:

can't	= cannot
won't	= will not
let's	= let us

they'd	= they would
he's	= he is, he has
who's	= who has, who is (not to be confused with whose, meaning "of whom")
it's	= it is, it has (not to be confused with its, the possessive)
o'clock	= of the clock
spit'n image	= spit and image

3) Plural of numbers, symbols or words used as terms

How many 10's did the ice-skater get?

His company prefers to hire only Ph.D.'s or M.A.'s.

The three *hors d'oeuvre* 's in the text were all spelled wrong.

♦ 9. Dash / Parentheses

A pair of dashes and a pair of parentheses let the writer insert a comment in text, with this difference: dashes emphasize the inserted material, and parentheses de-emphasize it:

My husband teaches ESL (English as a Second Language) in college.

She gave up volleyball (which she hated anyway) and happily switched to the swim team.

He looked innocent enough - and they never did prove anything in court - but Mark didn't trust him anyway.

— A single dash can also set off material, emphasize it, explain it, show hesitation, or otherwise mark it as special:

The host of the program explained how the product worked. how much it cost, how long it took if ordered by mail - everything except where to send for it.

Her youngest son, Henry, only weighs fifty pounds - all of it in perpetual motion.

Taken aback by the question, Mr. Szepanski cleared his throat and said, "I'm - we're - that is, I mean - can you repeat that, please?"

♦ 10. Brackets

Brackets act as parentheses within parentheses, or set off material within a quotation.

The government investigated several substances, (among them the much maligned monosodium glutamate [MSG]), and eventually proved most of them benign.

Staring into the camera as she stirred the mixture. she explained, "if you add it [the flour] too soon, it won't blend properly and the whole recipe will be ruined."

Essay
Pico Iyer

In Praise of the Humble Comma

The gods, they say, give breath, arid they take it away. But the same could be said – cculd it not? – of the humble comma. Add it to the present clause, and, of a sudden, the mind is, quite literally, given pause to think; take it out if you wish or forget it and the mind is deprived of a resting place. Yet still the comma gets no respect. It seems just a slip of a thing, a pedant's tick, a blip on the edge of our consciousness, a kind of printer's smudge almost. Small, we claim, is beautiful (especially in the age of the microchip). Yet what is so often used, and so rarely recalled, as the comma - unless it be breath itself?

Punctuation, one is taught, has a point: to keep up law and order. Punctuation marks are the road signs placed along the highway of our communication - to control speeds, provide directions and prevent head-on collisions. A period has the unblinking finality of a red light: the comma is a flashing yellow light that asks us only to slow down; and the semicolon is a stop sign that tells us to ease gradually to a halt, before gradually starting up again. By establishing the relations between words, punctuation establishes the relations between the people using words. That may be one reason why schoolteachers exalt it and lovers defy it ("We love each other and belong to each other let's don't ever hurt each other Nicole let's don't ever hurt each other," wrote Gary Gilmore to his girl-friend). A comma, he must have known, "separates inseparables," in the clinching words of H.W. Fowler, King of English Usage.

Punctuation, then, is a civic prop, a pillar that holds society upright. (A run-on sentence, its phrases piling up without division, is as unsightly as a sink piled high with dirty dishes.) Small wonder, then, that punctuation was one of the first proprieties of the Victorian age, the age of the corset, that the modernists threw off: the sexual revolution might be said to have begun when Joyce's Molly Bloom spilled out all her private thoughts is 36 pages of unbridled, almost unperioded and officially censored prose; and another rebellion was surely marked when E.E. Cummings first felt free to commit "God" to the lower case.

Punctuation thus becomes the signature of cultures. The hot--blooded Spaniard seems to be revealed in the passion and urgency of his doubled exclamation points and question marks ("¡Caramba! Quién sabe?"), while the impassive Chinese traditionally added to his so-called inscrutability by omitting directions from his ideograms. The anarchy and 'commotion of the '60s were given voice in the exploding exclamation marks, riotous capital letters and Day-Glo italics of Tom Wolfe's spray--paint prose; and in Communist societies, where the State is absolute, the dignity - and divinity of capital letters is reserved for Ministries, Sub-Committees and Secretariats.

Yet punctuation is something more than a culture's birthmark; it scores the music in our minds, gets our thoughts moving to the rhythm of our hearts. Punctuation is the notation in the sheet music of our words, telling us when to rest, or when to raise our voices; it acknowledges that the meaning of our discourse, as of any symphonic composition, lies not in the units but in the pauses, the pacing and the phrasing. Punctuation is the way one bats one's eyes, lowers one's voice or blushes demurely. Punctuation adjusts the tone and color and volume till the feeling comes into perfect focus: not disgust exactly, but distaste; not lust, or like, but love.

Punctuation, in short, gives us the human voice, and all the meanings that lie between the words. "You aren't young, are you?" loses its innocence when it loses the question mark. Every child knows the menace of a dropped apostrophe (the parent's "Don't do that" shifting into the more slowly enunciated "Do not do that"), and every believer, the ignominy of having his faith reduced to "faith." Add an exclamation point to "To be or not to be .. ." and the gloomy Dane has all the resolve he needs; add a comma, and the noble sobriety of "God save the Queen" become a cry of desperation bordering on double sacrilege.

Sometimes, of course, our markings may be simply a matter of aesthetics. Popping in a comma can be like slipping on the necklace that gives an outfit quiet elegance, or like catching the sound of running water that complements, as it completes, the silence of a Japanese landscape. When V.S. Naipaul, in his latest novel, writes, "He was a middle-aged man, with glasses," the first comma can seem a little precious. Yet it gives the description a spin, as well as a subtlety, that it otherwise lacks, and it shows that the glasses are not part of the middle-agedness, but something else.

Thus all these tiny scratches give us breadth and heft and depth. A world that has only periods is a world without inflections. It is a world without shade. It has a music without sharps and flats. It is a martial music. It has a jackboot rhythm. Words cannot bend and curve. A comma, by comparison, catches the gentle drift of the mind in thought, turning in on itself and back on itself, reversing, redoubling and returning along the course of its own sweet river music; while the semicolon brings clauses and thoughts together with all the silent discretion of a hostess arranging guests around her dinner table.

Punctuation, then, is a matter of care. Care for words, yes, but also, and more important, for what the words imply. Only a lover notices the small things: the way the afternoon light catches the nape of a neck, or how a strand of hair slips out from behind an ear, or the way a finger curls around a cup. And no one scans a letter so closely as a lover, searching for its small print, straining to hear its nuances, its gasps, its sighs and hesitations, poring over the secret messages that lie in every cadence. The difference between "Jane (whom I adore)" and "Jane, whom I adore," and the difference between them both and "Jane - whom I adore -" marks all the distance between ecstasy and heartache. "No iron can pierce the heart with such force as a period put at just the right place," in Isaac Babel's lovely words; a comma can let us hear a voice break, or a heart. Punctuation, in fact, is a labor of love. Which brings us back, in a way, to gods.

DIAGNOSTICS

PART V

✎ 40: Punctuation

Make all necessary changes in punctuation, or mark C if the sentence is correct as is.·

1. First of all we should discuss our present options.

2. Dorotea Munoz, head of the committee has proposed a solution.

3. Before we can begin please check to see that your packet, includes some paper, two pencils an evaluation form and a brochure.

4. If you think the Department has made a mistake, please indicate that by checking the box at the right.

5. I never thought Id see him again: however I must admit that thought gave me some pleasure.

6. When you go to the interview tomorrow, be sure to bring the following, a sharp pencil, a calculator and some graph paper.

7. The forest, bathed in the grayish haze of sunrise glowed with an intensity that promised a splendid summer day.

8. Before he even saw it Howie said; "That's the stupidest movie they ever made!

9. His "mansion on a lake" was nothing but a camper parked alongside a brackish pond.

10. With some trepidation she set the format inserted the diskette and pressed what she thought was the right key nothing happened.

✎ **41: Punctuation**

Insert all necessary punctuation in the following passage.

In actual fact the mountains of southern Poland arent very high She knew that from the research shed done But when Janina stepped out of the rental car she felt lightheaded She recognized it all the tiny village with its unpaved streets the geese that ran toward her honking the thatched cottages as if shed been there before In a sense she had Each time her grandmother had told her stories about when she was a girl Janina had pictured it exactly as she saw it today This is uncanny she mumbled out loud to herself Was there really such a thing as inherited memory

CONVENTIONS
or
The Parsley Sprig

When you serve your fine dinner, or your scrumptious dessert, there are always certain conventions to observe. Every culture has them. A parsley sprig on the platter, to embellish. A dollop of mint jelly next to the lamb. A little bit of sour cream served with your baked potato. These conventions are expected, and it just doesn't seem quite right if you ignore them.

It's the same with spelling. You could spell many English words differently and still pronounce them the same – for example, crazy / crazie / crazee would all sound the same, according to English phonetics. So what's the difference? What does it matter if you spell something wrong, if it sounds right anyway? After all, in the words of Andrew Jackson, "It's a damn poor mind indeed which can't think of at least two ways to spell any word."

Well, the difference is the same as if you served the mint jelly next to your baked potato. It just doesn't go together that way. Why not? Who's to say that you can't eat mint jelly on your baked potato?

Maybe you can – as an individual. Go ahead and put the cherry under the ice cream on your sundae at home; but when you serve one in public, if the cherry's not on top of the whipped cream, people will wonder why. Your credibility as a chef will suffer.

Rituals, like eating or language, don't depend on the individual. They get their form and substance from entire cultures. History. Cultural migrations. Mass agreement.

Conventions.

Most spellings in English come to us through hundreds and often thousands of years of historic blending and adaptation. Endings of words reflect that history, as do roots, prefixes, suffixes, etc. If you can remember some of the history, it'll stand you in good stead when you encounter an unfamiliar word with a familiar root.

That's basically what I want to do here: demystify spelling. Spelling is NOT as hard as you think. It's NOT as complicated as they taught you in school. You don't need to memorize as many rules as you tried to in school. Sound too simple? Let's see ....

Spelling Made Easy
(or at least a whole lot easier)

♦ 1. The Formula

The first thing you need to know, in order to master English spelling, is a rule that (so far) linguists have managed to keep to themselves. They know it, but somehow it doesn't seem to trickle down into the school curriculum anywhere. Which is a pity, since it explains so much of what can otherwise be perceived as crazy, English spelling.

Actually, it's more a formula than a rule, and it governs spelling in an almost mathematical fashion. I call it my **Spelling Formula**, and here it is:

1. $\bar{V}$ C V   2. $\breve{V}$ C C V

And here's what it means:

1. In any word, if you have the construction **Vowel - Consonant - Vowel,** the first vowel is long.

gāve   mōlehill   dīver

(if you're not 100% sure about long and short vowels, go back to Part I and review the Diagnostics and Practices. That concept is essential here.)

2. And if the construction in a word is **Vowel - Two Consonants - Vowel,** the first vowel is short.

lădder   wĭnning   cŏpper

It sounds simple, but this little Formula will help clear up many spelling questions that plague most people. Let's see how.

First, a question: Have you ever wondered why English has a silent E (like in "gate")? And if the silent E is important, why do you drop it when you add another syllable? Say these two words:

ăt   āte

What's the difference? Of course, it's the silent E. The only job of the silent E is to create the environment, or the

115

construction, of V-C-V, so the first vowel can be pronounced with a long sound.

If you're like most people, there are words that always give you trouble if you have to spell/write them. If I had a dime for each time I've seen the word "writting" on a student paper, I could retire!

What's wrong with "writting" — and how can you avoid similar mistakes? Remember:

V C V	V CC V

The verb is pronounced "rīt" (long I), which, according to the Formula V C V, means you must spell it "write." If you spell the gerund "writting," you've changed it to V CC V, so now - according to the Formula - you must pronounce it [rĭtting] (short I).

English has many such pairs of words, for example: diner/dinner, or later/latter. The only difference is the Formula, which, of course, makes all the difference in the world! Is the gerund form of the verb "shine" spelled "shining" or "shinning?" (Of course, it's "shining," which maintains the environment V-C-V, and thus the long sound).

This eliminates many of the uncertainties about English that we often go through life with. Try to remember some of the many wordy rules you had to memorize in school about spelling, that refer to words ending in -ing, -ed, final consonants, silent E..... If you apply the Formula, they all come down to a question of common sense.

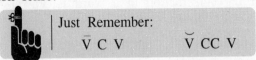

Just Remember:

$\bar{V}$ C V $\breve{V}$ CC V

Let's look at how this simple Formula replaces 3 unnecessary rules:

Rule #1. Double the final consonant before -ing, -ed, etc.

begin ⇒ beginning (V CC V, of course, to keep short I)

scrap ⇒ scraped (V CC V, to keep the short A sound) (not "scrapped", which would be V C V, long A)

Rule #2. Double the final consonant in longer words that end in a single vowel followed by a single consonant, where the stress falls on the last syllable.

commit ⇒ committed (otherwise, according to the VCV rule,
it would be pronounced with a long I ("mite")
upset ⇒ upsetting (otherwise, according to VCV, the ending would
sound like "seating")

Rule #3. Final consonants when preceded by two vowels are not doubled when adding a suffix that begins with a vowel.

beat   ⇒ beaten (the diphthong "ea" sounds like long E;
thus, "ea-t-e" = V-C-V)
soak ⇒ soaking (ditto: "oa" sounds like long O; hence, V-C-V)
retail ⇒ retailing (ditto: "ai" sounds like long A)
(The trick here is to think of a diphthong as one long vowel.)

I'm not saying that you should throw out all the spelling rules you learned. But as you can see, many of them are somewhat clumsy, wordy and complicated attempts to explain what the Formula explains so succinctly and easily. Those, you can forget!

And, of course, the Formula is even easier if you pronounce the word you're working on out loud, so you can hear the vowel sound. As you can see, clear, accurate pronunciation is extremely important to spelling!

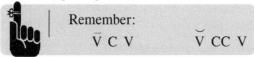

Remember:

V̄ C V   V̆ CC V

Let's look at a few more rules we can do without now. You'll find the following rules in most traditional grammar books, but they're all explained away by the Spelling Formula:

Rule #4. Words that end in silent E—omit the E before a suffix that begins with a vowel.

dine   ⇒ di**ni**ng (VCV)
desire ⇒ des**ir**able
trace ⇒ tr**ac**ing
write ⇒ wr**iti**ng (but: written, for short I)
please ⇒ pl**eas**ing (VCV, with a diphthong for the first
vowel)

With all these words, you no longer need the silent E, because it's been replaced by another vowel.

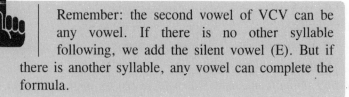

Remember: the second vowel of VCV can be any vowel. If there is no other syllable following, we add the silent vowel (E). But if there is another syllable, any vowel can complete the formula.

Rule 5. Words that end in silent E keep the E before a suffix that begins with a consonant.

hopeful	(of course; if you dropped the E, it would no longer be VCV, and therefore, not a long O)
sincerely	(ditto)
extremely	(VCV; otherwise -em would sound like it does in "empty"
lonely	(VCV; otherwise, the -on would sould like the word "on")
useful	(otherwise it would sound like "us")
ninety	(without the E-and VCV-here, you'd sound like a "ninny")

Some books even go so far as to list the following "exceptions" to that rule:

argument (not arguement)
truly (not truely)
duly (not duely)

But if you're familiar with the Formula, you know that these aren't exceptions at all. They simply follow the Formula. You no longer need the silent E's in these words, because any vowel (including Y) can complete the Formula. Just like you no longer need so many of the traditional "rules!"

♦ 2. The formula and Hard Consonants

(If you're not 100% sure about those, go back to Part I, Hard and Soft Consonants, and review the Diagnostics and Practices.)

What happens if you want to follow a hard consonant with a soft sound?

Remember: **hard** consonants are followed by the hard sounds **a, o or u.**

• if you're making a catalogue, are you cataloging or cataloguing?

• If you log an entry, are you loging, loguing or logging?

Many words that end in -log or -logue come to us from Greek by way of Latin (the Romans adapted many Greek words). The original words ended with -logus ("word"), and when they got translated into English, they kept the U and a silent E after the G.

That U is important. If you want to lengthen the word "log" (which comes to us from Middle English), for example, you have to double the G (to maintain the short O: V CC V): logging. But with words that came from Greek, they already have something after the G to keep it hard: the U. So instead of doubling the G, simply keep the original U: cataloguing (instead of "catalogging").

catalogue ⇒ catalogued

dialogue ⇒ dialoguing

You can think of the GU in these words as a doubled G. But why bother? Why not just double it, like English words, and be done with it? You will see these words spelled "catalog" and "dialog," just the way they sound. And that works just fine, until you want to add a syllable.

Words that come from Greek/Latin have the U after the G; words that come from English or Germanic languages (Anglo--Saxon) don't. The Anglo-Saxon words double the final G; the words with U don't need to. That's the only difference.

It's a question of history, and clarity. If you double the G ("catalogged, monologging"), you're stating by your spelling choice that these words have an Anglo-Saxon origin; but they don't. (If you're unsure about a word's origin, check the dictionary.) Spelling it "catalogging" seems as out-of-character as spelling the lumberjack's activity "Ioguing."

(This, by the way, is why we need the U in a word like "plague." Without the U after it, the -g- in the middle would sound like it does in the word "age." Don't forget to keep the U in extended forms like "plaguing," or "plagued.")

By the same token, words that end in C must also do something to maintain that hard sound when adding another syllable. Like with G, they add another letter: K.

picnic ⇒ picnicking
frolic ⇒ frolicked

You can think of this added K as doubling the hard C, since K and C are both representations of the same letter, one hard and one soft. What would happen if you simply doubled the C? You'd still have a C followed by a soft sound: "picnicced"; the C would still wind up being pronounced like an S.

So the Formula now liberates you from trying to remember all those rules about words like "picnic" and "dialogue/dialog".

Just remember: **V-CC-V**
(catalo-gu-ing; pla-gu-ed; lo-gg-ing...)
(pani-ck-ing; picni-ck-ed...)

As is the case with any language rule, there are exceptions to this **Spelling Formula.** But more often than not, you'll find that **V-C-V = V-CC-V** is an excellent general rule to follow that will help reason away many of your past spelling confusions.

♦ 3. The Shape-Shifters

(If you don't remember Schwa, go back to Part I and review.)

Unfortunately, the-sound of Schwa can be spelled with any vowel. So how do you know which one? There's no 100% rule, but this one will help in many cases.

For many years, I had trouble remembering the middle vowel in the word "med_cine." Then I discovered this rule:

When in doubt as to how to spell a schwa syllable, **change the word to a different form of the word** so that the stress falls on the schwa syllable.

Example: med?cine (N.) ⇒ medicinal (Adj.)

This shift in pronunciation highlights the former schwa syllable. Since I know how to pronounce the word "medicinal," this tells me which letter goes in the original word. You can do this with many words, for example:

profess?r (N.) ⇒ professorial (Adj.)

phot?graph (N.) ⇒ photography
(N.; not always another part of speech)

mel?dy (N.) ⇒ mel**o**dious (Adj.)

irrep?rable (Adj.) ⇒ rep**a**ir (V.)

incomp?rable (Adj.) ⇒ comp**a**re (V.)

adjud?cate (V) ⇒ jud**i**cious (Adj.)

Once you get the hang of it, this can be fun!

♦ 4. The Old Stand-by

Although we've now thrown out many of the so-called spelling "rules" that we learned in school, some of them have stood the test of time, and should be memorized. Here's one:

> I before E
> Except after C
> Or when sounded like A
> As in "neighbor" and "weigh"

Or its slightly altered version:

> I before E
> (Except after C)
> When it sounds like EE.

In other words, whenever the letters E and I are together in the same syllable, if they sound like EE (long E) the syllable's spelled "ie."

There are exceptions to this, but often it's because it's a foreign word and therefore doesn't follow English (British) rules: leisure (this follows the rule if you say it the British way, with a short E sound), (n)either (also follows the rule, British-style), sheik (an Arab word, really pronounced "shake", which follows the rule), financier (a French word), seize ....

but on the whole, a good rule-of-thumb.

♦ 5. More about Pronunciation

Spelling is directly affected by pronunciation. If you're not careful about your pronunciation, this can lead to errors, on your part or on the part of those listening to you. For example, if you always say "am**pi**theater" (instead of the correct form "amphitheater," with the diphthong), chances are pretty good that when it comes time to write it, you'll misspell it "ampi-."

Pay close attention to vowel sounds. They can help you (or those who depend on your words) avoid many spelling problems. If you pronounce words like **pin** and **pen** the same, or **sinner** and **center**, how will you – or the person listening to you -know how to spell it? (Context isn't always enough.) **Sit** is usually intransitive, but **set** is transitive; the pronunciation- makes all the difference. Saying it carefully helps you to spell it carefully.

There are many times when you can choose whether to be clear or unclear, just by your pronunciation. For example, if your listener can't tell whether you said **"inner**-office politics," **"intra**-office politics" or **"inter**-office politics," this could lead to confusion, especially if someone is taking notes and writing down your words. Is a City **Plan??er** a politician or a gardener (planter or planner)? Can you distinguish between **"sense"** and **"since?"** Do you hear a **C** and a **T** at the end of "district?" If not, someday you may misspell it the way it sounds in your head: district.

When you measure how much you weigh, you talk about your **weight** (rhymes with wait). But when you measure how tall you are, do you add an "h" to the word? Many people mispronounce that word "heigh**th**." Be careful: the word "height" ends with a **T**, not a **TH**. If you say "heighth," then by logic you should also say "weighth (waith)." And if you let yourself consistently pronounce it with a **TH** sound at the end, then when it's time to write it, you may misspell it accordingly.

Clearly, your pronunciation is a product of where you were raised. It varies from region to region. And just reading this isn't going to change the way you talk. But if you understand the phonetic principles at work and always try to pronounce your words clearly, paying careful attention to vowel and consonant sounds, your spelling will reflect this care. Spelling will get easier, and you'll be more successful at it.

♦ 6. The Ultimate Authority: the Dictionary

There's no spelling tool quite like the dictionary. If you're serious about mastering English, get yourself a good one. It can help you with pronunciation, spelling, derivation, roots and affixes, slang, history, and can be lots of fun to browse through.

You may even find, like the author, that it's downright difficult to look up a word — because of all the fascinating words you'll come across that distract you from your original mission!

See "Further Reading" at the back of this book for some suggestions of dictionaries and other books that will help you master this crazy language.

The Craziest Language

by

Abigail Van Buren

We'll begin with a box and the plural is boxes;

But the plural of ox should be oxen not oxes.

Then one fowl is a goose, but two are called geese,

Yet the plural of moose should never be meese.

You may find a lone mouse or a nest full of mice;

Yet the plural of house is houses, not hice.

If the plural of man is always called men

Why shouldn't the plural of pan be called pen?

If I spoke of my foot and show you my feet,

And I give you a boot, would a pair be called beet?

If one is a tooth and the whole set are teeth,

Why shouldn't the plural of booth be called beeth?

Then one may be that, and three would be those,

Yet hat in the plural would never be hose.

And the plural of cat is cats, not cose.

We speak of a brother and also of brethren,

But though we say mother, we never say methren.

Then the masculine pronouns are he, his and him,

But imagine the feminine she, shis and shim.

So English I fancy you will agree,

Is the craziest language you ever did see.

DIAGNOSTICS

PART VI

✎ 42: Spelling

Identify the spelling formula in effect in each word (VCV or VCCV).

1. latter	_____	11. surely	_____
2. open	_____	12. hotel	_____
3. translate	_____	13. bridal	_____
4. biting	_____	14. refusal	_____
5. hitting	_____	15. kennel	_____
6. driver	_____	16. strive	_____
7. happiness	_____	17. file	_____
8. shapely	_____	18. filler	_____
9. caped	_____	19. jolly	_____
10. capped	_____	20. thinning	_____

✎ 43: Spelling

Add "-ing" to the following words

1. spit _____
2. argue _____
3. choose _____
4. dine _____
5. occur _____
6. catalogue _____
7. contemplate _____
8. shine _____

9. panic _____

10. plague _____

✎ 44: Spelling

Find and correct the spelling errors in the following passage.

Before you go hikking in California, be sure everyone in your group is aware of the necessary precautions. Stay on marked trails and avoid touching unfamiliar plants; poisson oak is comon, and very unpleasant. Rattlesnakes are a fact of the Californian countryside, and they're most active during warm months. Although timid by nature, they will strike when unintentionally provoked. Watch where you step, don't overturn rocks (they may be sleeping underneath), and never put your hand in a spot you can't see (watch for toddlers, whose curiosity drives them to reach into every hole they see).

Always remember that California's dry, summer grasses are excellent tinder; any spark can set off a fire that can easyly become a disaster. Be sure you know park rules concerning barbecues and campfires.

And it's always a good idea to carry water; it's dry hiking out here, and with the strong sun shinning, you run the risk of dehydration. A hat will help, too.

Reprinted from SAN JOSE WITH KIDS by special permission.

PITFALLS

Every recipe has its little peculiarities. If you're making cookies, you can mix eggs and flour and sugar any old way; but if you're making home-made brownies, you have to add the ingredients in the right order or you wind up with a gluey mess that doesn't rise properly in the oven.

English has its little pitfalls, too. Most people have their own list of words they can't spell, or can't use correctly, or formulas they just can't remember. The rest of their language is pretty much okay, but when it comes to these problematic items, the system breaks down.

In this section, we'll look at some of those pitfalls. I hope some of your "favorite" ones are here; if not, let the publisher know so we can include them in the next edition.

❖ ❖ ❖

♦ ELUSIVE PAIRS

Since American English pronunciation is so lazy, with schwa's all over the place making things messy, many word pairs are unclear. Let's look at a few that give the most problems, either because of pronunciation or spelling. Wherever possible, the boldfaced letters indicate relationships between the words that can make them easier to remember.

If you understand fully the job of each part of speech, some elusive pairs become easier. (You might want to review Part II, Parts of Speech, before reading this section.)

Accept/except

- Accept =   verb (**A**ction word).
                  Don't accept his word on that.
- Except =   preposition.
                  They're all correct except the last one.

Advise/advice

- Advise - verb: Please advise me.
- Advice - noun: They gave us some **ni**ce ad**vice**.

127

Affect/effect

- Affect = verb (**A**ction word).
  Means "to have an effect on."
  This change will not affect your wages.
- Effect = noun. The effect is the result.
  This change will have no effect on your wages.
- Effect = verb. Means "to bring into Existence. To bring into existence means to make something BE, hence the E.
  This will effect great change in the company.

All ready/already

- All ready = adjective. If you can drop the "all" and make sense, then use this one; "ready" stands by itself here.
- Already = adverb: Are you all ready already?
  (adj)   (adv)

All together/altogether

- All together = adjective. Like "All ready," if you can drop the "all" and make sense, this is the one:
  They put the papers all together.
- Altogether = adverb.
  They have altogether too many papers.

Allude/elude/illusion

- Allude = make a reference to.
  He alluded to a Shakespeare play.
- Elude = Escape.
  The answer eludes me.
  Be careful when pronouncing the beginning vowels of:
    - illusion - make it sound like a short I. It shouldn't sound exactly like:
    - allusion - the act of alluding, or referring, to something
      (He made an allusion to the President's report)
    - elusive - pronounce the long E and it'll sound different from the other two beginnings.

The clearer your pronunciation, the easier it'll be to understand and the easier it gets to remember these elusive pairs.

Bath/bathe; Breath/breathe

- Bath/Breath = noun.
    Go take a bath. He took a deep breath.
- BathE/BreathE = vErb.
    Go bathe immediately. Breathe deeply.
    Memory jogger: The one with the **E** is the vErb

Between/Among

- Between - used between two items
    She split the remaining ice cream evenly between the two children.
    However. in some cases the underlying meaning is a doublet even though more than two are concerned:
    Between you, me and the lamppost.
    (The information in question is being shared between you and me. between you and the lamppost. and between the lamppost and me)
- Among - used for more than two.
    The prizes were divided equally among the four contestants.

Complement/compliment

- Complement = shares a common root with 'complete'
- Compliment = praise. civility

Conscience/conscious

- Conscience = noun;
    Listen to your conscience.
- Conscious - adjective:
    He was conscious when the ambulance arrived. [Remember: science is a noun; -scious is an adjective-ending suffix.)

Continual/continuous

- Continual means a repetitive action or pattern. not necessarily non-stop;
    A continual hammering (stop-start. stop-start. all day or all week long)
- Continuous means without stopping. without interruption.
    A continuous line (solid. unbroken)

Dessert/desert

- Dessert = Yum! 2 helpings, **2 S's**
- Desert = noun—sand; OR verb—to abandon:
  He deserted his battalion.
  To desert means 'to leave alone': one S 'alone'.

Do/due

- Do = verb:
  Go do your homework
- Due = adjective:
  The rent is due.

Does/dose

- Does = verb (3rd person -s ending) He does well in
  school.
- Dose = noun (or verb; medicinal)
  Be careful to take only the prescribed dose.

Imply/Infer

- Imply/Infer. The relationship between these words is that
  of cause and effect. If you imply something (the
  cause), I then infer what you mean (the effect).

It's/its

- It's = 2 words: it is. It's freezing today!
- Its = possessive Its cover was torn.

Led/lead

- Led = verb, past tense of LEAD (long E) He led the
  horses to pasture.·
- Lead = (short E) noun; a mEtAl The pipe is made of
  lead.

Lie/lay

- Lie = means to recline. Intransitive (never takes an
  object) Lie down on the couch.
  The book was lying on the table. Let sleeping dogs
  lie.
- Lie = means to tell an untruth. Intransitive.
  Don't lie to me.
- Lay = means to plAce or put. **Transitive** (always takes
  an object).

He lays carpet for a living. Harry is a brick layer
She laid the clothes on the bed.
The big problem with these two is in the past tense.
Consider these grids.

(Lie/lay coninued)
- **Present**

	to LIE		**to LAY**	

I lie	we lie	I lay	we lay
you lie	you lie	you lay	you lay
he, she, it lies	they lie	he, she, it lays	they lay

- **Past**

I lay	we lay	I laid	we laid
you lay	you lay	you laid	you laid
he, she, it lay	they lay	he, she, it laid	they laid

As you can see, the verb Lay is regular; that
is, it adds -d to form the past tense. Lie is
irregular, and in its past tense it looks like lay
in its present. Consider this past-tense sentence:

I lay down at ten, but I didn't fall asleep until
eleven thirty.

Like/as

- Like = preposition. In the manner of (followed by a
noun: Like a lady)
- As = conjunction, followed by a clause (subject and
verb): as you can see

Lose/loose

- Lose (soft S, like Z) = verb (remember that past, which
has one O: lost)
- Loose (hard S) -adjective

Migrate/emigrate/immigrate

- migrate = Latin, to move from one country/region to
another or to change location periodically.
- emigrate = Latin **ex**, out of = to come out of, to leave
a country

- immigrate = Latin, in, im, into = to move into, enter a country

  At the end of the 19th century, many residents of eastern Europe <u>emigrated</u> from their homelands where they suffered from poverty. They <u>immigrated</u> into the United States, forming one of the biggest <u>migrations</u> of population the world has ever ᴜ en.

Moral/morale

- Moral = (accent on the first syllable) 1. adjective

  It was a moral decision.

  2. noun: The story had an important moral (=lesson)

- Morale = (accent on the second syllable) noun. (mood; state of mental well-being).

  They threw a party to help boost morale.

Passed/past

- Passed = verb, regular -ed:

  I passed my exam.

- Past = adjective: past events

  or noun: He lives in the past.

Principle/principal

- Principle means a simple truth.
- Principal can be the Director of a school,

  The Principal is your pal

  or the amount of a loan.

Quit/quite/quiet

- Quit (short I) = verb

  He quit his job.

- Quite (long I) = adverb

  This is quite simple.

- Quiet = adjective (2 syllables like "silent")

  Be quiet!

Rise/raise

- Rise = Intransitive.

  The sun rises at five o'clock.

- Raise = Transitive (like lay).

  Raise the shades, please.

Memory jogger. lie ⎫
                rise ⎬ all **Intransitive**
                sit ⎭

(the other of each pair is transitive)

Sit/set

- Sit = Intransitive.

    Please sit over there.
    He sat on his hat.
    The transitive form is seat:
    The usher will seat people as they arrive.

(Sit/set continued)

- Set = Transitive (set what?)

    She set the alarm for six-thirty
    Memory jogger: In this set of 3 words — sit,
    seat, set — the two that have **E** in them are
    both transitive (take an objEct); the one that
    has an **I** is **I**ntransitive.

Than/Then

In common speech, they sound the same.'
Remember:

- Than is used with comparisons;
- Then refers to time.

There/their/they're

- *There* contains the word "here" and talks about location.
- *Their* contains the word "heir" and talks about
    ownership/possession.
- *They're* is two words: **they** and **are.**

We're/were/where

- We're = 2 words: **we** and **are**
- Were = past tense of BE, 3rd person plural
- Where = location; notice the word "here" in it

Who's/whose

- Who's = 2 words: **who is** or **who has**
- Whose = possessive.

    Whose book is this?

♦ DOUBLE NEGATIVE

Just like in math: a negative plus a negative equals a positive. Two negative words placed together change to a positive expression. **I don't have nothing** means I do have something. **He's not doing nothing** means he is doing something. Not nothing = something; not never = some time; etc. In other words,

"Don't never use two negatives in the same clause!"

It helps to understand what the negative words mean. Let's look at some of their definitions:

none	-	not one
never	-	not ever
nothing	-	no thing, not a thing
no-one	-	not a person, no one
nobody	-	no body, no person
nowhere	-	not anywhere, no place

The word "not" is already part of the negative word, so you don't need another in the sentence. Unless, of course, you mean a positive. For example:

He's not nobody, you know! (the speaker here is putting emphasis on the fact that he's somebody of importance).

Don't do nothing. (don't just sit there — do something!)

♦ UNNECESSARY PREPOSITIONS

The word **where** means **to** what place, **at** what place, etc. The preposition is included in the word "where," so you don't need another one.

✗ Where'd you get it at?
✔ Where'd you get it?

✗ Where's he going to?
✔ Where's he going?

♦ NON-PARALLEL STRUCTURE

English is a very harmonious language, in terms of structure. Words that join (conjunctions) always join balanced items. Sometimes, especially in longer sentences, it's easy to lose track of this balance, and if you do, your sentence will become awkward, although you may not be sure why.

Let's look at some examples of this imbalance, called non-parallel structure, and see how it can be avoided.

Pronouns - have you ever heard anyone say "for him and I"? Such a structure is unbalanced because it combines a subjective pronoun with an objective one. Use the same case on both sides of a conjunction joining pronouns.

The best way to keep compound pronouns balanced is to separate them (in your mind). **"For him and for I"?** Your ear knows you don't say "for I;" for is a preposition and must be followed by an object. A quick look at the pronoun charts will tell you that "me" is the objective pronoun for the first person singular, so it should be "for him and me."

Now fix these:

1) The couple sitting in front of Frank and I left during intermission.
2) He repeated it for the benefit of her and I.
3) I swore to her that him and I would never be friends again.

Answer : 1) The couple sitting in front of Frank and *me* left during intermission. 2) He repeated it for the benefit of her and *me*. 3) I swore to her that *he* and I would never be friends again.

Conjunctions - use the same grammatical structure on both sides of a conjunction (two clauses, two prepositional phrases, two gerunds, etc.)

✗ Call a friend from your class or who lives near-by.
✔ Call a friend who's in your class or who lives near-by.

✗ The job included typing, filling and I had to collect data.
✔ The job included typing, filling and collecting data.

✗ She had neither the money nor did she want to buy it.
✔ She had neither the money nor the desire to buy it.

Necessary Words – when you make the parallel elements similar in construction, be sure you include all the necessary words. Word order can also be important here. For example:

✗ We had to interview the parent of a student or a nurse.
(unclear: is the choice between a parent and a nurse, or between a parent of one and a parent of the other?)

✔ We had to interview the parent of a student or of a nurse.
✔ We had to interview a student's parent or a nurse.

♦ **LOOK-ALIKES**

Always be on the look-out for words that look exactly alike but are different parts of speech. They abound in English, and can fool you into using them incorrectly. For example:

fast   (adjective) = rapid.
He's a fast runner
(adjective) = attached.
The ship was fast (fastened) to the dock
(adverb) = quickly.
He ran as fast as he could.

found   (verb, present) = to establish.
She's going to found an orchestra.
(verb, past of "find")
They found the shipwrecked man.
(adjective) = unexpected.
He considered the found money a gift from fate.

will   (modal)
The concert will take place at eight o'clock.
(noun)
The dying man wrote his last will by hand.

Sometimes the pronunciation of these pairs is different, like in the words produce (noun: vegetables and fruit) and produce (verb: to make), or the pair līve (verb) and līve (adjective).

Often, though, the words are identical except for their part of speech, so the better you understand those, the easier it'll be to handle these pair words.

And sometimes, there's a form that sounds almost the same, but must be spelled differently. For example:

whip   (verb) = to flay.
It was common practice to whip young sailors.
(noun) = a long piece of leather.
He cracked the whip.

But if you mean the sweet stuff, be sure you add the past participle ending (-ed): Please pass the whipped cream. It sounds similar when said out loud, but must be spelled differently.

Another commonly misspelled pair is **suppose** (verb) and **supposed** (past participle as adjective).

      (verb) What do you suppose is the matter?

      (adj)   They were supposed to arrive an hour ago.

Here's a partial list of words that can be more than one part of speech. If you're not sure what their two (or more) parts of speech are, look them up in the dictionary. Then try to use them in a sentence of your own.

best	fence	grave	loom
boast	fill	hip	might
complex	find	hop	produce
dice	fly	knife	record
favor	graft	lash	returns

And, of course, if you're conversant in a foreign language, that gives you a distinct advantage in understanding these pairs of words (as well as a lot of other things in English). For example, the word **fast** translates into French as **rapide** (adj -rapid), **vite/ rapidement** (adv. -quickly) or attache (adj.-fastened). If you have the advantage of remembering the three different translations, it's impossible to confuse which is which, or how they should function in a sentence.

If, however, you're not conversant in another language, then you have to make a special effort to remember the part of speech in English. As you've seen before in the section on roots and affixes, knowing only one language can severely limit your full understanding of English.

♦ DANGLING MODIFIERS

A discussion of the structure of English sentences wouldn't be complete without mentioning these. A dangling modifier is a word, a phrase or an incomplete clause that doesn't modify anything in the sentence. It seems to, though, and that's the problem. Consider the following:

    Huffing and puffing, the stairway seemed endless.

Who was doing the huffing and puffing? The stairway? Obviously it's a person going up the stairway, but there is no person in the sentence; the intent is clear, but the grammar is murky. An adjective must modify a stated noun, but none is present here except "stairway".

Let's take a look at a few more, and see how they can be fixed.

✗ Standing on the corner, a sports car almost ran him down. (Was the sports car standing on the corner?)

✔ Standing on the corner, he was almost run down by a sports car.

✔ While he was standing on the corner, a sports car almost ran him down.

✗ Carefully, the eggs were blended into the mixture. (were the eggs careful, or someone else who isn't mentioned here?)

✔ Carefully, the cook stirred the eggs into the mixture.

✔ The eggs were blended carefully into the mixture.

✗ Sizzling loudly, Friedrich flipped the veal cutlets. (Was Friedrich sizzling?)

✔ Sizzling loudly, the veal cutlets were flipped.

✔ Friedrich flipped the sizzling veal cutlets.

♦ ODDS AND ENDS

Foreign Words — English uses many foreign words and abbreviations. Foreign words form their plurals differently than English words do, so you need to get familiar with some of the most common ones and their plural forms:

- **criterion** – Greek, from judge = a standard rule against which a judgement can be made. Plural: criteria (*Foreign words that end in -ion form their plural with -ia*)

- **curriculum** - Latin, course = course, class plan. Plural: curricula (*foreign words that end in -um form their plural with -a*)

- **datum** - Latin, something given = a given fact. Plural: data (*Data, meaning specific facts, is plural: The data are...; Data, meaning general information, is a singular collective noun: The data is ...*)

- **e.g.** – Latin, exempli gratia = for example.
- **etc.** – Latin, et cetera = and so on. Et means and, so never say "and etc."
- **i.e.** – Latin, id est = that is
- **N.B.** or n.b. - Latin, nota bene = note well, pay close attention to the following.
- **Schema** - Latin, form = diagram, outline or model. Plural: schemata

And don't forget to be wary of those tricksters in English, words that seem to mislead deliberately. In what other language would you drive on a parkway and park on a driveway? Where else besided English could you find a hamburger with no ham, an eggplant with no egg, a grapefruit with no grape, or a pineapple with neither pine nor apple in it?

Have fun!

ANSWERS TO DIAGNOSTICS

ANSWERS

♦ 1: Consonants

1. H	5. H	9. S	13. S	17. S
2. H	6. S	10. H	14. H	18. H
3. S	7. S	11. H	15. H	19. S
4. H	8. H	12. H	16. H	20. S

♦ 2: Vowels

1. S	3. L	5. L	7. L	9. S
2. S	4. L	6. S	8. S	10. L

♦ 3: Vowels

1. chocolate
2. correction
3. telephone
4. impeccable
5. organ
6. magazine
7. ability
8. telepathically
9. protozoa
10. metronome
11. gelatin
12. probability
13. larceny
14. segregation
15. chronological

♦ 4: Diphthongs

1. mealtime (V)
2. alphabet (C)
3. impeach (V), (C)
4. hourglass (V)
5. anthem (C)
6. crushing (C)
7. reproach (V), (C)
8. sharpening (C)
9. poolhall (V)
10. unbelievable (V)
11. entertainment (V)
12. congealed (V)
13. auditory (V)
14. ashen (C)
15. proud (V)

♦ 5. Vowels

Pronunciation is a tricky thing in English.
schwa S (long e)L D   S schwa   S (long e)   S   S   S

You probably know a lot of it without
D   S schwa (long e)   L   schwa S   schwa S   S   D

thĭnkĭng abŏut ĭt, bŭt the rĕst bears stŭdȳ.
S   S   schwa D   S   S   schwa S   D   S (long e)

Whĕn you've mastĕred the sŏunds of the
S   D   S schwa   schwa D   schwa schwa

lĕtters, you'll bē readȳ tō gō ŏn tō the
S schwa   D   L   D (long)(long u) L   S (long u) schwa

nĕxt sĕctĭon of the bŏok.
S   S   D Schwa Schwa D.

♦ **6: Nouns**

1) C 2) P 3) C 4) Cl 5) P 6) C 7) Cl 8) P 9) Cl 10) P

♦ **7: Nouns**

1) M 2) C 3) M 4) C 5) M 6) C 7) M 8) M 9) C 10) C

♦ **8: Nouns**

1. fewer cavities
2. how many
3. fewer calories
4. C
5. a few of the people

6. fewer than seven
7. greatest number
8. so few tourists
9. the next year, the fewest
10. fewer attendance hours

♦ **9: Nouns**

1) <u>Mr. Bukowski,</u> <u>our esteemed colleague</u> was the man responsible for this new system of accounting.

2) He thought of <u>Uncle Ted,</u> <u>his mentor and teacher,</u> and wished he were there.

3) One of her fondest dreams was to be like <u>Mrs. Fitzpatrick,</u> <u>her first-grade teacher.</u>

4) I'd always hated studying <u>grammar,</u> a dry boring set of rules, until I met <u>Mr. Atsuyama,</u> my college English teacher.

5) All the employees in the office got together and wrote a joint, co-signed letter to <u>Harris Forbes,</u> <u>the founder of the magazine</u> (that had lambasted their firm).

6) <u>Red</u>, <u>a primary colour</u> makes the flowers in this landscape stand out brilliantly.

7) For their homework, which was usually quite substantial, they only had to look up some facts in <u>Dog Fancy</u>, <u>a magazine devoted to dogs and people who love them.</u>

8) <u>The fact</u> that you didn't finsih the job doesn't look good on your résumé.

9) Last weekend, I went to a ball-game with <u>my friend</u> Juendan.

10) I'll never forget the day I first saw <u>Elsie the Cow</u>, (or: <u>Elsie the Cow</u>), <u>the mascot for Borden's Milk Company</u>!

♦ **10: Nouns**

1) Where did Mom put the <u>cookie</u> <u>dough</u>?

2) <u>Paper</u> dolls were lying all over the floor, and Katie sat in front of her <u>doll</u> <u>house</u> cutting out more.

3) I didn't feel good, so I went to the store to get some <u>headache medicine.</u>

4) <u>Computer</u> programming is the job of the future.

5) Sabjali Hassan, a <u>newspaper</u> <u>reporter</u> from Madagascar, was working for a year at the New York Times as part of a professional exchange.

6) The highly-paid speaker called their city a <u>cow</u> <u>town</u>, offending all the civic leaders in the <u>conference</u> <u>room</u>.

7) The loud noise startled Millie, causing her to spill the <u>cake</u> <u>mix</u> all over the <u>marble</u> <u>counter</u> <u>top</u>.

8) The <u>door</u> <u>handle</u> fell off in his hands, and his impetus made him topple back onto the <u>porch</u> <u>railing</u>.

9) When the encyclopedia <u>salesman</u> ran down the front steps, chased by the barking dog, he tripped and fell over the garden <u>hose</u> that lay curled up on the lawn.

10. One of the hardiest of all breeds, the Alaskan <u>sled</u> <u>dog</u> often sleeps under a mound of snow that falls on him during the arctic night.

♦ 11. Articles

1) It is <u>the</u> decision of <u>the</u> Board that all employees on <u>the</u> Retirement Plan are eligible for <u>an</u> interest-bearing retirement account at <u>a</u> bank of their choice.
2) <u>The</u> platypus is <u>an</u> animal indigenous to Australia.
3) If you mix <u>a</u> half-pound of butter with <u>an</u> ounce of chocolate and <u>a</u> cup of sugar, <u>the</u> result is delicious!
4) Where's <u>the</u> sign-in book? Over there, on <u>the</u> counter.
5) Which is heavier, <u>a</u> pound of feathers or <u>a</u> pound of gold?

♦ 12: Pronouns

1) **I** - 1st person singular, nominative (subject); **her** - 3rd person singular, objective; **they** - 3rd person plural, nominative (subject)
2) **You** - 2nd person singular or plural, nominative (subject); **them** - 3rd person plural, objective; **they** - 3rd person plural, nominative (subject).
3) **they** - 3rd pers. pl., nom. (sub.); **each other** - (3rd pers.) reciprocal.
4) **them** - 3rd pers. pl., obj.; **me** - 1st pers. sing., obj.; **They** -3rd pers. pl., nom. (sub.)
5) **it** - 3rd pers. sing., nom. (sub).; **it** - 3rd pers. sing., obj.
6) **we** - 1st pers. pl., nom. (sub.); **one another** - (1st pers.) recip.
7) **I** - 1st pers. sing., nom. (sub.); **something** - 3rd pers. sing., indef.; nom. **it** - 3rd pers. sing., nom. (sub.); **that** - 3rd pers. sing., indef., obj.
8) **you** - 2nd pers. sing. or pl., nom. (sub.); **these** - demonstrative pl., obj.; **those** - demon. pl., obj.

9) **ones** - 3rd pers. pl., indef., nom.; **that** - relative, nom.
10) **which** - relative, obj.; **us-** 1st pers. pl., obj.

♦ 13: Pronouns

"When we arrive at the hotel, Marcia, you and John set up the tables first. Cover **them** with the linen cloths, white on the bottom and the pink ones on top, laid out on the bias.

"Carmen, you and Mike will take care of setting out the meats. You can each do one table. John can help you when he's finished covering tables. **He** and Marcia are just here for the day, so they'll help out wherever they can.

"Vladimir, get **those** trays of glasses out of the back of the truck; you can set them up in pyramids, like you did at the last job. That was beautiful!

"Anna, once the tables are covered and the casseroles are out, start setting out the rest of the food. You'll have some help from Vladimir and **me**, once I've finished talking with the bride's mother.

"Now, I want ice around all the cheeses, the soft stuff, all the perishables. Vladimir, you're the one **who** is responsible for that. Keep that ice coming! When it starts to melt, or if people take it for their drinks, keep refilling it."

♦ 14. Adjectives

1) deafening (G); old (A)
2) exciting (G); summer (AN)
3) remarkable (A); developmental (A); baby's (PA); early (A)
4) this (DA); floor-based (Part A); activity (AN); perfect (A); little (A)
5) amber (A); grain (AN); gentle (A); morning (AN)
6) your (PA); little (A)
7) her (PA); coffee (AN); kitchen (AN)
8) ineffective (A); best (A); their (PA)
9) little (A); adorable (A); little (A); pink (A); blue (A); fuzzy (A)
10) small (A); fresh (A); summer (AN); ripe (A); aromatic (A); green (A); red (A); dwarf (A); fruit (AN); laden (A); bowed (Part A)

♦ 15: Adverbs

1) well, often
2) slowly, carefully
3) ill
4) steadily, weakly, quickly
5) badly, nicely
6) illegibly, barely
7) hardly
8) hard, often
9) esthetically, politically
10) vociferously, morally

♦ 16: Adjectives and Adverbs

As they descended the walkway, the sights and sounds of the Moroccan city assailed their senses. They both walked more and more slowly, as the crowd surged around them and the other passengers, almost impeding all movement. Men in burnooses, small boys peddling their cousin's hotel, women selling jewelry (probably stolen jewelry, she thought), they all covered the stone pier. Elbowing their way through the mass of people as quickly as they could, Elsa and Robert finally stepped onto the mainland. Elsa felt unsettled, as if she'd been plunked down on a different planet. Haughty-looking camels waited, their halters held by disinterested-looking men. From somewhere nearby, coffee smelled strong on the morning air. A wave of nausea came over Elsa, striking her unexpectedly, without warning. But even as she fought it, she knew that here in Tangiers she would find what she'd set out to find. Life was treating her well.

♦ 17: Prepositions

1) over, through, to
2) over, around
3) under, for
4) in, around
5) behind, of, back, forth, up, down
6) to, toward
7) across, to
8) Underneath, to
9) on, under
10) within, of, about, on, outside, to, of, on

♦ 18: Conjunctions

1) but
2) and
3) becuase
4) if
5) Neither ... nor
6) when
7) and, while, and
8) and, or, if, however, while
9) when
10) although

◆ 19: Roots

1) script - write
2) port - carry
3) cred - believe
4) swim - to propel oneself through the water
5) put - to place
6) bio - life
7) fortuna - chance
8) grad - step
9) vis - able to be seen, to see
10) muni - city, town

◆ 20: Prefixes

1) inter - into
2) pro - for
3) re - back
4) anti - against
5) cor (con) - with
6) de - away
7) ex - out of
8) re - back
9) in - not
10) omni - all

◆ 21: Suffixes

1) tion - noun ending
2) less - without
3) ly - adverb ending
4) ity - noun ending
5) ness - noun ending
6) ious - adjective ending
7) logy - study of
8) ment - noun ending
9) ist - one who
10) er - one who

◆ 22: Roots and Affixes

1) con (with), tact (touch) = to touch, get in touch with
2) ad (next to), junct (join) = someone or something joined to someone/thing else
3) puni (punish), tive (adj. ending) = something/someone that punishes
4) contra (against, preventing), cept (birth), ive (adj.) = something that prevents birth
5) ex (out of), tract (pull), ion (noun ending) = pulling out of
6) arbor (tree), ist (person who ...) = person who takes care of trees
7) im (not), penetr- (go through), able (capable of) = unable to be pierced/penetrated
8) ex (out), pul (push), sion (noun ending) = pushing or throwing out
9) e (out), ject (throw), ion (noun ending) = throwing out

10) syn (same), chron (time), ize (verb ending) = to make or change to the same time.

◆ 23: Word Families

1) colony, colonist
2) routinely
3) frighten
4) heavily
5) imagination
6) floral
7) enrage
8) frightfully, frighteningly
9) uniquely
10) circular

◆ 24. Parts of Speech

1) V, Adj
2) V, N
3) V, N, Adj
4) V, N
5) V, N
6) N, Adj.
7) V, N
8) V, N, Adj.
9) V, N
10) V, N, Adj.

◆ 25: Verbs

1) sat (T, A), streamed (T, A)
2) will be marked (T, P)
3) rose (T, A), had (T, A)
4) gave (T, A), permeated (T, A)
5) will have been taken over (T, P)
6) was (C), had gotten (T, A), looked (C)
7) am ('m) (C), doesn't seem (C)
8) is (C), smells (C)
9) don't think (T, A), are (C), feel (C), fit (T, A)
10) had been pounded (T, P), was (C)

◆ 26: Verbs

1) to be - inf.; not to be - inf.
2) slipping - ger.;, sliding - ger.
3) to go - inf.
4) to include - inf., procrastinating - ger.
5) to have - inf.; to get - inf.; dieting - ger.
6) to turn out - inf.; resulting - ger.; staffing - ger.
7) to gain - inf.; funding - ger.; staffing - ger.
8) to request - inf.; carrying out - ger.
9) seeing - ger.; believing - ger.; to think - inf.
10) sightreading - ger.; accompanying - ger.; performing - ger.; to master - inf.

♦ **27: Verbs**

1) Have-aux.; seen-main
2) know-main; have-aux.; been-main
3) 've (have)-aux.; skied-main; haven't-aux; lived-main
4) hasn't-aux; seen-main; 'm (am)-main; 'll - aux (modal); be-main; 'd (had)-aux; written-main
5) Are-aux; putting-main; are-aux; coming-main
6) don't-aux; know-main; get-main; am-main; do aux; know main
7) is-aux; planning-main; 's (is)-aux; having-main
8) said-main; haven't-aux; finished-main; should -aux (modal); wait-main; have-main
9) can - aux (modal); bet - main; haven't -aux; heard - main; 've (have) - aux; run-main; have - aux; changed - main.
10) is-main; 's (has) aux; won-main; don't-aux; know-main.

♦ **28: Verbs**

1) is - simple present indicative
2) 've ... been - pres. perfect indicative; 've ... seen - pres. perf. ind.
3) will help - future
4) came - simple past; saw - simp. past; conquered - simp. past
5) Go - pres. imperative; see - pres. imp.
6) had...abated past perfect ind.; finished - simp. past
7) would ... have done - conditional perf.
8) will help - future; 've (have) understood - pres. perf.
9) were - past subjunctive.
10) have ... seen - pres. perf.

♦ **29: Verbs**

1) must
2) should
3) could
4) can
5) might
6) would(n't)
7) should
8) ought
9) can't, would
10) might

♦ **30: Verbs**

1) turned-I; blared-I
2) stared-I; executed-T

3) rinsed-T; filled-T; shook out-T
4) have fallen-I; survive-T; 'll (will) ... rise-I
5) played-I; lingered-I; would start-I
6) will meet-I; go over-T (or "go-I")
7) placed-T; swept-I
8) had thought-I; cut-T; ensnared-T
9) cut-T; disappeared-I; sped-I; began-T (object; "swimming")
10) procrastinated-I; made-T; 'h (had)... finished-T; didn't have-T (object: "to do it"); wanted-T; had-T; didn't have-T (obj.: "to hand it in").

♦ 31: Parts of Speech

The <u>airplane</u> <u>rose</u> sharply, climbing <u>to</u> an altitude of 30,000 feet.
    Noun Verb   Prep
Below <u>the</u> wing, <u>she</u> could see the cities of <u>Sacramento</u> <u>and</u>
     Art   Pro   Proper Noun Conj
West Sacramento stretching across the <u>flat</u> plains <u>along</u> <u>its</u> two
                             Adj   Prep Poss adj
rivers, the Sacramento and the American. To the north, rice
fields <u>glistened</u> <u>brightly</u> in the sun. <u>They</u> looked like huge squares
      Verb   Adv   Pro
<u>and</u> rectangles of ice, or <u>gigantic</u> mirrors. <u>Dipping</u> <u>sharply</u> to
Conj   Adj   Ger   Adv
the right, the plane banked and turned, and <u>finally</u>, covering
                                  Adv
the brilliant sun with a wing, <u>it</u> <u>straightened</u> and headed like an
                       Pro   Verb
arrow toward the <u>snow-capped</u> Sierra Nevada, <u>the</u> towering
               Adj   Art
<u>mountains</u> to the east.
  Noun

♦ 32: Phrases and Clauses

1) P	3) C	5) P	7) P, C	9) P
2) C	4) P	6) C	8) C	10) P

♦ 33: Phrases and Clauses

1) her impudent son (Noun, object of verb "sent"); to his room (Prep., Adv.); without his supper (Prep., Adv.)
2) The little boy (Noun, Sun); shouted and waved (Verb); his voice (Noun, Sub); over the roar (Prep.); of the surf (Prep.)

3) for a joke (Prep., Adv.)
4) The two tomcats (Noun, Sub); hissing and snarling (Ger., Adj.)
5) Laughing and crying (Ger., Adj.); the two old friends (Noun); at the same time (Prep., Adv.); into each other's arms (Prep., Adv.)
6) for a few minutes (Prep., Adv.)
7) Two hundred soldiers (Noun, subject); off to battle (Prep., Adv.); of the bagpiper (Prep., Adj.)
8) After the movie (Prep., Adv.); to the little café (Prep., Adv.); on the square (Prep;, Adj.); with their dessert (Prep., Adv.)
9) on a large, flat rock (Prep., Adv.); the young girl (Noun, subject); her bare feet (Noun, object of verb); in the icy water (Prep., Adv.)
10) The deer (Noun, sub.); at the top (Prep., Adv.); of the ravine (Prep., Adj.); about their footing (Prep., Adv.); about the two strange, two-footed creatures (Prep., Adv.); –also: the two strange, two-footed creatures (Noun, obj. of Prep.); from the other side (Prep., Adv.)

♦ 34: Phrases and Clauses

As the last two people took their seats, a hush fell
      noun phrase
over the expectant audience. Someone coughed.
  prepositional phrase   clause
When the conductor raised her baton, it was as if
        clause
the whole audience released the collective breath they'd
        clause
been holding. Violins and violas began suddenly, followed by
      noun phrase
the basses. The timpani crashed and rumbled, and without
      verb phrase
warning, out of nowhere, the eerie vibration of a gong rang
    prepositional phrase
out over the music. The sound of the strings diminished until
they were barely audible. Trombones and trumpet took up
    adjective phrase

the melody <u>after that,</u> playing with a vigor and volume that
         adverbial prep. phrase
made the <u>listeners' seats</u> vibrate
          noun phrase

♦ 35: Phrases and Clauses

1) That's the road (Ind); that we should have taken (Dep).
2) I need the umbrella (Ind); that's in the closet (Dep).
3) The road isn't always the best (Ind); that's the straightest (Dep).
4) This place has the best food (Ind); I've ever tasted (Dep).
5) Did you see the sign (Ind); that said there was a detour (Dep).
6) They asked for our passports (Ind); which we didn't have with us (Dep).
7) The boy missed all the excitement (Ind); who was asleep in the back seat (Dep).
8) John Sutter died a poor man (Ind); who owned the mill (Dep); where gold was discovered in California (Dep).
9) In order to maximize profits, we shall have to abandon the project (Ind); (that) we began last quarter (Dep).
10) The cows will soon be moving up to higher ground (Ind); that are in the lower pasture (Dep); that's still snow-covered (Dep).

♦ 36: Sentence

1) <u>You</u> <u>don't have</u> any money.
  (sub)   (verb)

2) <u>You</u> <u>are going</u> to the party on Friday.
  (sub)   (verb)

3) <u>That package</u> <u>hasn't arrived</u> yet.
    (sub)   (verb)

4) <u>They</u> <u>are going to be finished</u> by tomorrow, or
  (sub)   (verb)

   I <u>shall come back</u> next week.
  (sub)   (verb)

5) I <u>should have called</u> sooner.
  (sub)   (verb)

6) <u>Freedom of speech</u> <u>is</u> one of the most important
      (sub)   (V)
rights we have.

7) If <u>you're going to be</u> late, <u>you</u> <u>should(n't) call and let</u> them
      (sub)   (verb)   (sub)   (V-compound)
know.

8) <u>They</u> <u>would have gone</u> anyway, even if <u>they</u> <u>had known</u>.
  (sub)   (verb)   (sub)   (verb)

9) <u>That painting</u> <u>is</u> in which museum (?)
     (sub)   (V)

10. <u>You</u> <u>(do) believe</u> in extra-terrestrial life.
   (sub)   (verb)

♦ **37: Sentence**

1) S	3) S	5) S	7) C-Cx	9) C
2) C	4) C	6) Cx	8) S	10) S

♦ **38: Sentence**

1) I	3) I	5) I	7) S	9) S
2) Imp	4) S	6) Imp	8) I	10) Imp

♦ **39: Sentences**

1) S/I
2) S/I (with compound verb)
3) Cd/I
4) S/I (interrogative)
5) Cx/I
6) Cd-Cx/I
7) Cd-Cx/I
8) S/Sub
9) Cd/I
10) S/I

♦ **Punctuation (First paragraph from Part V)**

If you wanted, you could take everything you've learned so far and put it together any way you wanted. Theoretically, anyone would understand you(,) since the words are all **there** in the **right** order. **O**rder is everything, right? **W**ell, no. **I**n language, like in many things in life, attention to detail makes all the difference.

♦ **40: Punctuation**

1. First of all, we should discuss our present options.
2. Dorotea Munoz, head of the committee, has proposed a solution.

ANSWERS

3. Before we can begin, please check to see that your packet includes some paper, two pencils, an evaluation form(,) and a brochure.
4. C
5. I never thought I'd see him again; however, I must admit that thought gave me some pleasure.
6. When you go to the interview tomorrow, be sure to bring the following: a sharp pencil, a calculator(,) and some graph paper.
7. The forest, bathed the grayish haze of sunrise, glowed with an intensity that promised a splendid summer day.
8. Before he even saw it, Howie said, "That's the stupidest movie they ever made!"
9. C
10. With some trepidation, she set the format, inserted the diskette, and pressed what she thought was the right key; nothing happened.

ANSWERS

♦ 41: Punctuation

In actual fact, the mountains of southern Poland aren't very high. She knew that from the research she'd done. But when Janina stepped out of the rental car, she felt lightheaded (or: light-headed). She recognized it all — the tiny village with its unpaved streets, the geese that ran toward her honking, the thatched cottages – as if she'd been there before. In a sense, she had. Each time her grandmother had told her stories about when she was a girl, Janina had pictured it exactly as she saw it today. "This is uncanny!" (or: "This is uncanny.") She mumbled out loud to herself. Was there really such a thing as inherited memory?

♦ 42: Spelling

1) VCCV	5) VCCV	9) VCV	13) VCV	17) VCV
2) VCV	6) VCV	10) VCCV	14) VCV	18) VCCV
3) VCV	7) VCCV	11) VCV	15) VCCV	19) VCCV
4) VCV	8) VCV	12) VCV	16) VCV	20) VCCV

♦ 43: Spelling

1. spitting
2. arguing
6. cataloguing
7. contemplating

3. choosing   8. shining
4. dining   9. panicking
5. acknowledging   10. plaguing

♦ 44: Spelling

Before you go <u>hiking</u> in California, be sure everyone in your group is aware of the necessary precautions. Stay on marked trails and avoid touching unfamiliar plants; <u>poison</u> oak is <u>common</u>, and very unpleasant. Rattlesnakes are a fact of the Californian countryside, and they're most active during warm months. Although timid by nature, they will strike when unintentionally provoked. Watch where you step, don't overturn rocks (they may be <u>sleeping</u> underneath), and never put your hand in a spot you can't see (watch for toddlers, whose <u>curiosity</u> drives them to reach into every hole they see).

Always remember that California's dry, summer grasses are excellent tinder; any spark can set off a fire that can <u>easily</u> become a disaster. Be sure you know park rules concerning barbecues and campfires.

And it's always a good idea to carry water; it's dry hiking out here, and with the strong sun <u>shining</u>, you run the risk of dehydration. A hat will help, too.

PRACTICES

These exercises will give you more practice in the topics tested in Diagnostics. Answers follow this section.

PART I

Practice 1: Consonants

Write **H** if the **bold-faced** letter is hard, and **S** if it 's soft.

___ 1. stuck	___ 8. plagiarism	___ 15. spices
___ 2. confused	___ 9. caption	___ 16. funny
___ 3. ingest	___ 10. insist	___ 17. target
___ 4. coward	___ 11. computer	___ 18. misery
___ 5. proceed	___ 12. enraged	___ 19. frolicsome
___ 6. sister	___ 13. seeing	___ 20. gifted
___ 7. golf	___ 14. visit	

Practice 2: Vowels

Write L if the bold-faced vowel is long, and S if it's short.

___ 1. capacity	___ 8. fallacious	___ 15. possible
___ 2. funnel	___ 9. infinite	___ 16. genes
___ 3. infused	___ 10. continent	___ 17. concluding
___ 4. automotive	___ 11. decrepit	___ 18. concussion
___ 5. Peter	___ 12. total	___ 19. defined
___ 6. winning	___ 13. indelible	___ 20. impale
___ 7. findings	___ 14. tractor	

Practice 3: Vowels

Underline the vowel that's pronounced with the "schwa" sound.

1. impossible	8. talent	15. additional
2. automobile	9. travel	16. factual
3. filtration	10. database	17. competition
4. delicious	11. typography	18. collect
5. telepath	12. correction	19. confuse
6. intelligent	13. saxophone	20. commonly
7. commodious	14. correspond	

Practice 4: Diphthongs

Underline the diphthong, and label it V for vowel or C for consonant.

___ 1. noisy   ___ 8. streamer   ___ 15. fourth
___ 2. mailman   ___ 9. changeable   ___ 16. antifreeze
___ 3. threaten   ___ 10. heiress   ___ 17. notebook
___ 4. staircase   ___ 11. wealthier   ___ 18. scholarship
___ 5. Athens   ___ 12. checkers   ___ 19. ninth
___ 6. triumph   ___ 13. quaint   ___ 20. shortcomings
___ 7. makeshift   ___ 14. poultry

Practice 5: Pronunciation Review

Underline all vowel sounds in the following sentences, and indicate whether it's long (–), short (◡), schwa (S) or a diphthong (D).

1. Mine is on the table.
2. Don't be late to class.
3. Air fills your lungs every time you breathe.
4. Millions of people live in China.
5. Better late than never, but better never be late.
6. Thousands of students attended the conference.
7. If she doesn't finish her homework by tomorrow, she'll fail.
8. The beautiful scene made me nostalgic.
9. "He's winning!" cried the lone spectator.
10. Wagons creaked and groaned, slipping along in the ruts etched in the soft rock trail.

PART II

Practice 5: Pronunciation Review

Write C for common, P for proper and Cl for collective.

___ 1. computer   ___ 11. Faculty
___ 2. articles   ___ 12. Intelligence
___ 3. Shakespeare   ___ 13. United Nations
___ 4. country   ___ 14. explanation
___ 5. Parliament   ___ 15. the Senate
___ 6. Morocco   ___ 16. joystick
___ 7. tea leaves   ___ 17. idea
___ 8. Congress   ___ 18. the navy
___ 9. recipe   ___ 19. Old Ironsides
___ 10. cartography   ___ 20. Beethoven

Practice 7: Nouns

Write C for a count noun and M for a mass (non-count) noun.

___ 1. tablecloth	___ 8. program	___ 15. folder
___ 2. bottle	___ 9. uranium	___ 16. dust
___ 3. pollen	___ 10. sea salt	___ 17. petals
___ 4. ounce	___ 11. seashell	___ 18. styrofoam
___ 5. powder	___ 12. bleach	___ 19. pine needles
___ 6. geraniums	___ 13. clouds	___ 20. teacher
___ 7. antenna	___ 14. vapor	

Practice 8: Nouns

Correct any count/mass nouns used incorrectly. Write C if the sentence is correct as is.

1. By the end of the game, Paul had less marbles than Cary.
2. Bruno knew this road had much more turns than the other.
3. By the time they'd finished dinner, Alex had the least peas left on his plate.
4. He ate so much cake at the party that when he got home he was sick.
5. Which class had the least failing grades?
6. Don't eat too much of those cherries.
7. The dinners on the left page of the menu come with less side dishes than the dinners on the right page.
8. Francois understood less of the lecture than Adrien did.
9. The college she finally chose was a good one, but it offered less choices of major areas of study.
10. By the time he was six, Josef spoke English with much more fluency than either of his parents.

Practice 9: Nouns

Underline the noun (or noun phrase) once and its appositive (noun in apposition) twice.

1. John Bettincourt, an outstanding athlete, played baseball in the spring and football in the winter.
2. Both Mark and his brother Alan will attend Yale in the fall.
3. Children taking violin lessons often enjoy playing "Twinkle,

Twinkle, Little Star: a piece known throughout France as a famous children's folk song.

4. I always look forward to driving on Highway 1, a road with spectacular ocean views.
5. San Francisco, a city built on seven hills, reminds many people of Rome.
6. On the poster, which was cracked and peeling off the brown bricks, he read the name of Don Manuel Garda, the famous flamenco dancer from Granada, Spain.
7. All the guests sat patiently waiting for Wanda's famous dessert, the best apple pie in the whole village of Wola Mielecka.
8. I'd like you to meet Chuck Cartelli, author of "Pasta and More." one of the best books on Italian cooking that you'll ever find.
9. One of his heroes was Scott Joplin. composer of hundreds of lovely rag-time piano pieces that have been popular since the end of the nineteenth century.
10. In the wild west, the frontier of the young United States, women were scarce and schooling was usually at a bare minimum.

Practice 10: Nouns

Draw two lines under each <u>adjectival noun</u> and one line under the <u>noun</u> that it modifies.

1. The pool water was a constant 80 degrees fahrenheit.
2. Our math teacher was so nervous about his class observation that he left his lesson plan at home.
3. It seems that soda machine works better after a firm kick.
4. Two fat hens and one colorful rooster raced around the chicken coop squawking and scratching.
5. During the course of the weekly budget meeting, Mr. Chen. the financial counselor assigned to our unit, offered some important suggestions about our company 5 money management.
6. She flung her pencil case at the door in anger, but her older brother slipped out just in time.

7. The plant holder came equipped with a black light to enhance growth and an instruction booklet that explained the use of the unusual light.

8. On the neat wooden table sat a ceramic cookie jar full of aromatic cookies, and a matching sugar bowl and creamer.

9. Watermelon rinds lay all over the kitchen counter, and seeds were strewn across the shiny linoleum floor, glistening wet and impossible to pick up.

10. When they arrived at their hotel, the company had sent a fruit basket and some cut flowers to welcome them to their temporary home.

Practice 11: Articles

Underline all articles.

1. All of the new diskettes have been put in a box labeled "Diskettes - New" on top of the Main Counter.

2. If any of the ingredients are left out, the result will be a sticky, awful-tasting mess.

3. Before leaving for the beach, be sure you have your bathing suit, a beach towel, at least one good book, and a sandwich or a snack.

4. He sat on the museum bench, staring at the huge, overpowering painting, awed by the colors and the sense of urgency they created.

5. English 52 is already filled, but by the time you go to register, they might have opened up a new class or two.

Practice 12: Pronouns

Underline all pronouns and indicate person, number and case or type.

1. Henry fully intended to let them know of his decision, but by the time he'd made up his mind to go tell someone in the office, they'd all gone home.

2. It's important that you study critically everything I teach you in this class, you're not here to meekly accept what is given, but to question it.

3. You tell someone and he tells someone else, and that's how gossip travels.

4. Who knows what he or she really wants in this life?

5. The ones in the red bin cost $1.50, and those over there, on the counter, cost $2.00; which would you like?

6. Did you see that? He sawed his assistant in half, and then she got up and did it to him.

7. They quizzed each other on what they'd learned in class that day.

8. Don't put that there, it's too heavy.

9. No one could possibly have guessed what he'd had in mind when he gathered them together.

10. We need to think of ourselves sometimes, to the exclusion of all others, because nobody else really knows what we need.

Practice 13: Adjective

1) Underline all adjectives. 2) Indicate adjective (A), gerund adjective (G), adjectival noun (AN), participial adjective (Part A), possessive adjective (PA) or demonstrative adjective (DA) for each one.

1. The scribbled note was almost impossible to read, even with her powerful magnifying glass.

2. Crushed or dried garlic will do in this recipe, but chopped, fresh garlic is much better.

3. What did you do with that aluminum foil I bought at the new supermarket this morning?

4. Flying squirrels are not often seen around here, but if you're patient. you might get to see the tree squirrel that often plays around that big tree over there.

5. The earthenware bowl, dripping with melted chocolate, sat in the sink waiting to be washed, but before she ran the water into it, her two children dipped their hands into it and licked all the chocolate off the edges.

6. Karl had already talked to his landlady, and the same detective that had been there yesterday was planning on a repeat visit this afternoon, unaware of Karl's plan.

7. To prepare for her demonstration of the winning original recipe, she assembled carefully all the necessary ingredients: sliced green peppers and eggplant, chopped celery, several tomatoes cut up, a diced onion, grated garlic, and some cheese she'd already grated beforehand.

8. During the wedding, crying babies and fidgeting children distracted everyone from concentrating on the beautiful ceremony, but the bride was truly delighted that all the young children in the large family were able to be there for her special day, and to her the crying was delightful music.

9. A strange little brown bird perched on the highest branch, singing a lively song that Giuseppe had never heard in all his young life.

10. Plaintive and reed-like, the sounds of the bag-pipe sliced through the evening calm, piercing in quality, reminding Sean of his summers in the highlands.

Practice 14: Adverbs

Underline all adverbs.

1. Do your work as well and as quickly as you can.

2. Internet allows you to communicate globally from your own home computer.

3. She laughed loudly and wholeheartedly, and the infectious sound soon had the whole roomful of nervous students giggling.

4. The brownies disappeared faster than any other dessert on the table, and Maria rushed back and forth to the kitchen with the tray, replenishing the ever-dwindling supply.

5. Ordinarily we don't meet so often, but the project we're currently working on is more complex and seems to require our getting together more frequently.

6. The folding chairs were all stacked precariously, forming a very unstable tower of black and beige.

7. He swallowed drily and took two steps backward, until he felt the cold, brick wall against his back.

8. The door clanged shut heavily, echoing weirdly through the large, barn-like room like a metallic thunder-clap.

9. The youth grabbed wildly at the branches that hung out over the rushing river, gasping fiercely for air and screaming for help.

10. "Get out!" she yelled sharply, picking up a book and hurling it viciously at his head.

PRACTICES

Practice 15: Adjectives and Adverbs

Identify the adjectives and adverbs in the following sentences.

1. He answered timidly, but his answer was correct.
2. Your youngest son is quite tall for his age.
3. The stupid computer's broken again!
4. The silver key goes to the red car, but the other one is very old and serves no useful purpose.
5. Stir the garlic and butter quickly as you add the vegetables, so that they don't get too hot too fast.
6. In the black box she found a small ring, whose stones glowed brightly under the strong lamp.
7. The speaker pointed importantly at the boring charts he'd brought, and a loud snore suddenly broke the heavy tension in the room.
8. Seated at her window, Severine could faintly hear the mournful, haunting chords of a Chopin nocturne, played slowly and with extraordinary depth of feeling.
9. She hinted vaguely that she was too tired to continue.
10. The cake rose fast in the hot oven, golden and fragrant, and Claudia removed it quickly, gently closing the oven door with her foot.

Practice 16: Prepositions

Underline all prepositions in the following sentences.

1. This letter should be forwarded to the payroll office, with the appropriate forms.
2. The information was faxed to our office by the president pro tem, indicating to all concerned that they were to continue following the usual procedure but that all memos would now be routed through the secretary's office.
3. He ran through the doorway and dashed up the stairs. calling to his friend as he ran.
4. Everywhere she looked there were clothes - on every table, under the chairs, draped across the couch, even hanging over the lamp.

5. Brilliant sunlight streamed through the window, slashed into blinding slices by the Venetian blinds, illuminating tiny, dancing motes of dust.

6. She wrote the sentence on the blackboard, drawing a line under all the prepositions.

7. Darting and weaving, the kittens ran around the bush and climbed up the tree, jumping from branch to branch until they finally leapt onto the roof of the garage.

8. Holding the envelope to the light, Benoit tried to discern the amount on the line and the signature scrawled across the bottom.

9. She stopped typing, hands poised over the keyboard, and listened again for the faint sound, her heart thumping wildly against her chest.

10. Clementine's ball of yarn rolled off her lap, bounced against the bag that was propped up at her feet, and continued rolling slowly out of the open door and onto the landing.

Practice 17: Conjunctions

Underline all conjunctions.

1. If you ever need help, don't hesitate to call and we'll send someone right away.

2. Let us know when you get there, and we'll send a car to meet you.

3. Either they take the offer we made them, or we just forget about the whole deal.

4. Take it or leave it!

5. In a mixture of this sort, the results can be quite surprising, therefore, I must stress again that everyone using the lab today must wear protective goggles.

6. They didn't take either the money or the food we left them, but I bet they took both the radio and the car keys.

7. Whales are mammals, like humans, and although they live in water, they breathe air, moreover, they bear their young ones and produce milk to feed them.

8. In 1998, if all goes well, my brother will finish college, but

he plans on going a fifth year to graduate school while he looks for jobs in his field.

9. Since I haven't finished the manuscript yet, the printer can't begin his work and the typographer will have to work overtime all next week.

10. The sauce isn't ready yet, so don't boil the spaghetti yet.

Practice 18: Roots and Affixes

Underline the root of each of the following words and give its meaning.

1. indescribable ⎯⎯⎯⎯⎯   11. predictable ⎯⎯⎯⎯⎯
2. operator ⎯⎯⎯⎯⎯   12. runner ⎯⎯⎯⎯⎯
3. construction ⎯⎯⎯⎯⎯   13. correction ⎯⎯⎯⎯⎯
4. incendiary ⎯⎯⎯⎯⎯   14. inequitably ⎯⎯⎯⎯⎯
5. indivisible ⎯⎯⎯⎯⎯   15. refrigerate ⎯⎯⎯⎯⎯
6. translucent ⎯⎯⎯⎯⎯   16. contents ⎯⎯⎯⎯⎯
7. transportation ⎯⎯⎯⎯⎯   17. vendor ⎯⎯⎯⎯⎯
8. nutrition ⎯⎯⎯⎯⎯   18. bakery ⎯⎯⎯⎯⎯
9. concentrate ⎯⎯⎯⎯⎯   19. studious ⎯⎯⎯⎯⎯
10. untenable ⎯⎯⎯⎯⎯   20. recipient ⎯⎯⎯⎯⎯

Practice 19: More Fun with Roots and Affixes ...

Underline the root of each of the following words and give its meaning.

1. education ⎯⎯⎯⎯⎯   11. technology ⎯⎯⎯⎯⎯
2. eminent ⎯⎯⎯⎯⎯   12. revitalize ⎯⎯⎯⎯⎯
3. inflammatory ⎯⎯⎯⎯⎯   13. retraction ⎯⎯⎯⎯⎯
4. fratricide ⎯⎯⎯⎯⎯   14. hypercritical ⎯⎯⎯⎯⎯
5. incandescence ⎯⎯⎯⎯⎯   15. unannounced ⎯⎯⎯⎯⎯
6. municipality ⎯⎯⎯⎯⎯   16. approbation ⎯⎯⎯⎯⎯
7. nascent ⎯⎯⎯⎯⎯   17. cartographic ⎯⎯⎯⎯⎯
8. cognizant ⎯⎯⎯⎯⎯   18. incantation ⎯⎯⎯⎯⎯
9. spatial ⎯⎯⎯⎯⎯   19. chronology ⎯⎯⎯⎯⎯
10. abundant ⎯⎯⎯⎯⎯   20. radical ⎯⎯⎯⎯⎯

PRACTICES

Practice 20: Prefixes

Underline the prefix in each of the following words and give its meaning.

1. automatic	_____	11. unable	_____
2. polyunsaturated	_____	12. microchip	_____
3. synthetic	_____	13. biodegradable	_____
4. antipathy	_____	14. patricide	_____
5. rewritten	_____	15. retrospect	_____
6. unsatisfied	_____	16. multipurpose	_____
7. antisocial	_____	17. deflate	_____
8. antecedent	_____	18. ethnocentric	_____
9. congenital	_____	19. expatriate	_____
10. enable	_____	20. transmit	_____

Practice 21: Suffixes

Underline the suffix in each of the following words and give its meaning.

1. musician	_____	11. antifungal	_____
2. naturally	_____	12. pesticide	_____
3. abundant	_____	13. convivial	_____
4. toasty	_____	14. turbulence	_____
5. information	_____	15. vendor	_____
6. meaningful	_____	16. altruism	_____
7. requisite	_____	17. prohibit	_____
8. refrigerator	_____	18. studious	_____
9. partial	_____	19. invisible	_____
10. oppressive	_____	20. containment	_____

PRACTICES

Practice 22: Roots and Affixes

Separate the following words into its roots and affixes.

1. desperation	11. microorganism
2. reactionary	12. counterproductive
3. misanthropy	13. transportation
4. prenatal	14. compelling
5. contraceptive	15. serrated
6. automotive	16. detachable

7. sequel
8. remake
9. arboreal
10. aviation

17. misinformed
18. telescopic
19. incomprehensible
20. antidisestablishmentarianism

Practice 23: Word Families
Change the following words to the part of speech indicated.

1. curious ⇒ N
2. tenacity ⇒ Adj
3. marriage ⇒ V
4. infinity ⇒ Adv
5. unfortunate ⇒ N

6. monster ⇒ Adj
7. ability ⇒ V
8. derive ⇒ N
9. musical ⇒ Adv
10. tightly ⇒ V

Practice 24: Verbs
Underline each verb, and indicate whether it's a True verb or a Copula, and if True, whether it's Active or Passive.

1. If you're really quick, you can see the coyote as it comes around that outcropping.
2. The old carpet had been used for so many years that the floor boards could be seen in a line from one door to the other.
3. Her grandson climbed up on her lap, threw his arms around her neck, and grinned mischievously.
4. Flags flapped in the breeze as fireworks exploded high over the lake.
5. The water for the noodles was boiling over, but as he reached for the lid, the pot-holder he was holding was pulled out of his grip when it snagged on another pot handle.
6. It fell into the pot of sauce, and as it hit with a loud splat, orange-colored sauce splattered all over the counter and the floor.
7. The boy took aim, closed one eye and pulled the trigger: one duck was clearly hit, and another began to fall but pulled back out of its dive and continued flying.
8. If you submit the application by Friday, there's still time; it can be processed by Admissions next week, and you should

be informed of their decision by the Registrar in early January.

9. By the end of this school year, Marius will have been in this country for over a year.

10. My teacher's been honored with an award for excellent teaching, and I heard that a wonderful speech was given by the President of the college at the awards ceremony.

Practice 25: Verbs

Identify all infinitives and gerunds.

1. When parking on a hill, it's important to engage the parking brake and to turn the wheels toward the curb.

2. Honking and flapping their wings, the gaggle of geese ran after the unknown visitor, forcing him to turn and run back towards the woods and abandon all hope of approaching the house.

3. Don't blame me if you forget to turn off the power and there's a short circuit.

4. When she was little, she learned to play the accordion and the piano, and now whenever they're having a party at the dorm, they call on her to play and liven things up.

5. If you insist on doing it yourself, at least let me give you some pointers on avoiding mishaps.

6. Before adding the flour to the banana mixture, pour a few drops of vinegar into a third of a cup of milk (to make it sour), and let it sit while you continue adding the other ingredients.

7. As soon as class was finished, the two friends went swimming in their favorite swimming hole, but since they forgot to bring towels, they dried off by chasing each other around the water's edge.

8. Cooking can be very relaxing, especially if you have a good friend to help you eat the results.

9. If you enjoy snorkeling, you have to visit the Great Barrier Reef off Australia, which offers some of the best fish viewing in the world.

10. After drifting, unsure and unsettled, for so many years, Oskar finally decided to settle down, to finish his studies, and to find himself a good woman to share the rest of his life with.

Practice 26: Verbs

Label all auxiliary verbs and main verbs.

1. "Have you ever tasted vanilla-flavored tea?" she asked her guests as she put the kettle on.

2. The sled was flying downhill faster, faster, picking up speed as it sped past trees and rocks, and soon it was heading for the fence that surrounded the parking area at the bottom of the hill.

3. If you had never seen the sign, I could understand your actions, but you knew it was there as well as I did.

4. I thought they would have already finished priming and painting the whole exterior by now, but as it turns out, they haven't even started painting yet.

5. Even though she can hardly afford food and clothes for all her kids, she's planning on buying a computer so she can start a business at home.

6. You haven't lived until you've skied in the Alps!

7. Once you've added the spices and the sauce is bubbling, you don't want to forget to keep stirring.

8. Antonia had never heard a mandolin until she visited her grandparents in Naples.

9. Just about everyone in the class has already had the chickenpox, but I'm not sure if the teacher's had it.

10. He didn't do it! I saw the whole thing, and just like I've told the police, he didn't do any of what they say he's done!

Practice 27: Verbs

Name the tense and mood of each verb.

1. Water boils at a lower temperature at higher elevations.

2. Many terms in cooking, like in music, come from French or Italian.

3. If I were a millionaire, I'd buy my daughter a horse, something she's wanted all her life.

4. Before that day, Jake had never tasted hominy grits or fried chittlin's.

5. Get off that couch and get to work!

6. All of you gathered here today are, without a doubt, incensed by what you've heard on the radio and seen on television; well, ladies and gentlemen, so are we, yes, so are we, and I hope that after this meeting we will have done something about it.

7. Sir, if you don't mind, please let me see one of those watches, there, the gold one with the tiny diamonds.

8. I remind you again, everyone, that it is absolutely essential that no one get word about this deal until the papers are signed by their lawyers.

9. While she was playing the piano, she lost all track of time and place and was transported to a world entirely of her own imagination.

10. If only people could get along without fighting!

Practice 28: Verbs

Underline all modals.

1. They couldn't stay awake while they studied. so they decided they would make a pot of coffee.

2. "You ought to do it up right: he drawled, before spitting in the sand.

3. He can't afford his car payments, so he definitely shouldn't plan on taking a vacation this year.

4. Nutrition experts agree that Americans should eat less red meat, and I think everyone here must agree that we should certainly cut back on salty junk food.

5. 'Can I go, Mommy, please, can I, can I?"
   "May I. You know you should say 'May I' when you're asking permission.

6. Many people feel that the government ought to be less involved in our lives; my husband believes it should be more involved but in fewer areas.

7. Can you play the piano?

8. So let's get started now, shall we?
9. If she thinks I shouldn't put so much salt in the food I cook, in my house, then she should stay home and cook her own food!
10. The announcer on the radio said we might have a storm this evening. but it looks as if it may start raining sooner than that.

Practice 29: Verbs

Underline each verb. and write T for Transitive and I for Intransitive.

___ 1. Crack the eggs with care, and if any of the shell falls in, remove it carefully.

___ 2. He said he wanted to take a shower before leaving the house.

___ 3. IIe said he's a cowboy, and that he breaks horses for a ranch about fifty miles from here.

___ 4. "I came, I saw, I conquered" is a famous quote attributed to Julius Caesar.

___ 5. Francesco never eats lasagna, but he's crazy about cannelloni.

___ 6. Publishing is a time-consuming business that requires long hours, intense dedication and lots of imagination and up-front money.

___ 7. If you intend to prepare the whole dinner yourself, get an apron and go to it.

___ 8. When we're in kindergarten, we learn to listen to those older than us, to hold hands, to tell the truth, and to share; all in all, that's not bad advice for us older folks to take to heart, too.

___ 9. The sound of horses' hooves thundered across the prairie, and the herd kicked up a dust storm that was visible for miles in each direction.

___ 10. My son loves computer games. and can spend hours at them; my daughter, on the other hand, is perfectly content to sit with a good book for hour after hour.

PART III

Practice 30: Phrases and Clauses

Write P for each phrase and C for each clause.

____ 1. humming to himself and smiling broadly

____ 2. it's snowing

____ 3. that they bought yesterday at the mall

____ 4. he was humming to himself and smiling broadly

5. the long, blue and white one in the hall closet

____ 6. mazurkas are usually written in three-four time

____ 7. sweet and sour sauce with the pork and lobster sauce with the shrimp.

____ 8. beaten physically, perhaps, but with spirit intact

____ 9. let's eat

____ 10. brimming over with kindness and beaming a radiant smile

Practice 31: Phrases and Clauses

Underline all phrases and indicate their type. Remember; some can fit more than one category.

1. Do this for me: put your name at the top of the page, look at the test paper, and decide how much of it you can answer with certainty.

2. The PTA were excited at the opportunity to have a real, live author come and talk to the classes.

3. Bugs covered the outside of the screen, making rasping noises that Jill found irritating.

4. He played all kinds of music on only a saw and a comb, and his audience was enthralled by it.

5. The orchestra played music of Tchaikovsky and Beethoven, and ended their outdoor concert with a rousing rendition of Handel's Royal Fireworks Music accompanied by real fireworks.

6. The two little boys rolled down the same grassy hill, over and over, tumbling over each other and rolling head over heels, and when they tried to stand up they were so dizzy

that they fell back down, clutching the ground and laughing until their sides hurt.

7. Mai Yee stopped eating, her chopsticks poised in the air, and without a sound she rose from her seat by the window and sped to the door to intercept the messenger.

8. Once the mayonnaise is added to the sauce. the rest of the ingredients have to be added immediately, or the whole mixture will soon begin to turn into a brown, gooey mess.

9. Buying his first car was the beginning of John's new life of independence.

10. Her goal was to be the best darned first-grade teacher that Clanton, Mississippi had ever seen.

Practice 32: Phrases and Clauses

Underline all <u>Independent Clauses</u> once and <u>Dependent Clauses</u> twice.

1. The books we borrowed yesterday have to be returned to the library by March first.

2. Chicken is one type of meat that must be kept well chilled until use.

3. My kids won't eat any sauce that has vegetables in it.

4. Generally speaking, kids who are expected to do well in school by their parents usually wind up doing just that.

5. Mr. Ashkenazy plays Rachmaninoff with a depth of expression that I've never heard before in a pianist.

6. When the rice mixture that's browning in the pan begins to sizzle, pour in the water I've already measured into the cup over there.

7. Old Faithful is a geyser in Yellowstone National Park that erupts once every hour.

8. Although all his colleagues defended cases that brought them bundles of money and renown, Jake always preferred representing people in court who otherwise could never afford a decent lawyer.

9. In her whole life she'd never seen such a mess; everywhere she looked there were piles of stuff, mountains of junk he'd probably never used and probably didn't even know was there.

10. Eyes closed as if in prayer, Agniezka was lost in the amazing variations of sounds she was able to produce on the ancient organ.

Practice 33: Phrases and Clauses

In the following passage, locate and identify all the: 1) prepositional phrases, 2) independent clauses, and 3) dependent clauses.

Far below Mount Fuji, nestled between its plain and the rugged sea, sits the town of Numazu. It lies at the convergence of three, fault lines, and often shakes as the earth struggles to release its pressure. In this town of a thousand pines, Marcella lived with her daughter, Claudia. Every day, they walked from their little apartment near the railroad tracks to the tiny road that led up the mountain called Kanukiyama. As they began their ascent, they would stop at the little stone shrine. Claudia enjoyed the colorful flowers that someone always kept in small vases next to it. Then they would walk, slowly, slowly, up the winding road, stopping only once they'd reached the old pagoda. When Claudia squealed at the sight of the funny hens and noisy roosters that lived next to the pagoda, Marcella knew they were there. Each time, they spent at least an hour playing on the slide in the little playground, and then, after visiting the pagoda, they began their slow walk back down the mountain.

Practice 34: Sentences

Change each question to a statement. changing any necessary words or expressions, and indicate the subject and verb.

1. Do you want to come with us to the beach?
2. What language are they speaking?
3. Haven't you ever heard of comparative linguistics?
4. Did you say that the report won't be ready until Friday?
5. Are those cookies for someone in particular?
6. Is your Dad coming to the Father-Daughter Dance with you, or is he going to be out of town?
7. Do you think they meant what they said?
8. Won't they ever change their minds?

PRACTICES

9. Hasn't she seen that movie already?

10. Do you have any game programs on your computer at home?

Practice 35: Sentences

Write **S** for simple, **C** for compound, **Cx** for complex or **C-Cx** for a compound-complex sentence.

1. In fourteen hundred and ninety-two, Columbus sailed the ocean blue.

2. Aunt Helen worked in the kitchen quietly, moving back and forth from counter to stove to sink, humming to herself occasionally but for the most part just silently concentrating on her cooking and the two delicious pies on the counter in varying stages of completion.

3. Sit down and eat your peas, and I don't want another word out of you.

4. Did you want the one that has the ribbon on top?

5. They sat together on the porch, listening to the night sounds; in the yard, their two grandsons ran through the tall grass catching fireflies.

6. Henceforward, all such requests will be routed through Mr. Henderson's office, and only the ones he personally okays will go upstairs.

7. They each threw a rock into the cave, and suddenly a million (or so it seemed) bats came swooping out into the evening air, making a frightening rustling sound with their wings.

8. They dived behind the bushes, and covered their heads with their hands.

9. Don't you sass me, young man!

10. I'd like one head of lettuce, a bunch of broccoli, a bag of yellow onions, and if it's not too much trouble, could you reach up on top there and get me that nice bouquet of flowers that has the shiny ribbon around it?

Practice 36: Sentences

Write **I** for indicative, **Imp** for imperative, or **S** for subjunctive.

_____ 1. Put on some music with dinner, darling.

_____ 2. If he didn't have his computer games, Alexander would die of boredom during the summer.

_____ 3. Putting money in an individual retirement account is an investment in your own future.

_____ 4. If only we were rich enough to afford a down payment!

_____ 5. Mr. Zukowski, sir, I called you because this customer insists that we refund his money without a receipt.

_____ 6. With an eerie, almost melancholy quality to it, music wafted to her ears from the stereo in the living room, blending with the night sounds that surrounded the terrace where she sat.

_____ 7. In order to make a truly outstanding pizza, it is important that you start with a fresh crust and home-made sauce.

_____ 8. I already gave you my telephone number, didn't I?

_____ 9. One of the elephants at the Sacramento Zoo died last year, and they can't keep the other one there because elephants are social animals and can't live alone.

_____ 10. Did you know that if you blindfold someone and give them fresh slices of apple and of potato to taste, they can't tell the difference?

PART V

Practice 37: Punctuation

Make all necessary changes in punctuation, or mark C if the sentence is correct as is.

1. "Hey, you" cried the shopkeeper, "come back here."!

2. In her class on world literature, she studied works by Chekov; Shakespeare; Twain and Zola.

3. If they dont' have garlic just buy the onions and the oregano.

4. Mrs. Chiangs' neighbors always barbecued on Fridays and once in a while when they didn't have too many people over they asked her to join them.

5. A marsupial is an animal that carries its young in a pouch they're almost all indigenous to Australia although North America has one the opossum.
6. The Sousaphone a variation of the tuba, was named for John Phillip Sousa a world-famous American composer of marches.
7. Picture this; six open-topped train cars in a row each one with a giraffe's head a real one sticking out the top.
8. In order, to prepare for his university year abroad, Andrew made sure he had: a passport, two pairs of solid walking shoes, an umbrella, and gifts, for his host family.
9. If you want to invent a new recipe, you have to be absolutely sure what each of the ingredients does if not you can wind up with something quite different from what you had in mind.
10. My mother-in-laws' driving is awful her rapidly-failing vision makes her reaction time dangerously slow.

PRACTICES

Practice 38: Punctuation

Punctuate the following passage.

How important were the missions to California Open up a map Those words may look like city names but before there was a city there the name was already in place from Basilica San Diego de Alcala in the south all the way up past San Francisco de Asis and a few more along the way Santa Barbara San Luis Obispo Is there a big city missing Not really Before it became the City of the Angels Los Angeles belonged to an archangel San Gabriel and the mission named for him sat at the crossroads of the west coast of America

Brian Bates. Excerpt from SAN JOSE with KIDS. Reprinted by permission.

Practice 39: Spelling

Identify the spelling formula in effect in each word (**VCV** or **VCCV**).

____ 1. happen ____ 11. cupid
____ 2. shining ____ 12. carbonated
____ 3. holler ____ 13. utter
____ 4. hemmed ____ 14. channel

_____ 5. shatter   _____ 15. hammer
_____ 6. thrice   _____ 16. Danish
_____ 7. shilling   _____ 17. while
_____ 8. compute   _____ 18. copper
_____ 9. belated   _____ 19. dialogue
_____10. voting   _____ 20. amusing

Practice 40: Spelling

Add "-ing" to the following words.

1. fly _____   11. review _____
2. whine _____   12. abut _____
3. side _____   13. whittle _____
4. swim _____   14. shun _____
5. jog _____   15. commune _____
6. whip _____   16. bat _____
7. thrill _____   17. judge _____
8. reveal _____   18. time _____
9. don _____   19. peruse _____
10. slice _____   20. imitate _____

PRACTICES

ANSWERS TO PRACTICES

Practice 1: Consonants

1. H	5. S	9. H	13. H	17. H
2. S	6. H	10. H	14. S	18. S
3. S	7. H	11. H	15. S	19. H
4. H	8. S	12. S	16. H	20. H

Practice 2: Vowels

1. S	5. L	9. S	13. S	17. L
2. S	6. S	10. S	14. S	18. S
3. L	7. L	11. S	15. S	19. L
4. L	8. L	12. L	16. L	20. L

Practice 3: Vowels

1. impossible
2. automobile
3. filtration
4. delicious
5. telepath
6. intelligent
7. commodious
8. talent
9. travel
10. database
11. typography
12. correction
13. saxophone
14. correspond
15. additional
16. factual
17. competition
18. collect
19. confuse
20. commonly

Practice 4: Diphthongs

1. noisy (V)
2. mailman (V)
3. threaten (C, V)
4. staircase (V)
5. Athens (C)
6. triumph (C)
7. makeshift (C)
8. streamer (V)
9. changeable (C)
10. heiress (V)
11. wealthier (V, C)
12. checkers (C)
13. quaint (V)
14. poultry (V)
15. fourth (V, C)
16. antifreeze (V)
17. notebook (V)
18. scholarship (C, C)
19. ninth (C)
20. shortcomings (C)

Practice 5 Pronunciation Review

1. Mīne ĭs ŏn the tāble
          s   s
2. Dōnt't bē lāte to clăss
                   s

3. Air fills your lungs each time you breathe.
  D   D   D   D   D

4. Millions of people live in China.
   D/S   S   D   S   S

5. Better late than never, but better never be late.
   S   S   S   S   S

6. Thousands of students attended the conference.
   D S   S   S   S   S   S S

7. If she hasn't finished her homework by tomorrow, she'll fail.
                 S   S   S   D

8. The beautiful scene made me nostalgic.
  S   D   S S

9. "He's winning!" cried the lone spectator.
            S   S

10. Wagons creaked and groaned, slipping along in the ruts
     S   D   D   S   S

    etched in the soft rock trail.
      S   D

Part II

Practice 6: Nouns

1. C	5. P, Cl	9. C	13. P	17. C
2. C	6. P	10. C	14. C	18. Cl
3. P	7. C	11. Cl	15. P, Cl	19. P
4. C	8. P, Cl	12. C	16. C	20. P

Practice 7: Nouns

1. C	5. M	9. M	13. C	17. C
2. C	6. C	10. M	14. M	18. M
3. M	7. C	11. C	15. C	19. C
4. C	8. C	12. M	16. M	20. C

Practice 8: Nouns

1. fewer marbles
2. many more turns
3. the fewest peas
4. C
5. fewest failing grades
6. too many of those cherries
7. fewer side dishes
8. C
9. fewer choices
10. C

Practice 9 : Nouns

1. <u>John Bettincourt</u>, an <u>outstanding athlete</u>, played baseball in the spring and football in the winter.

2. Both Mark and his <u>brother Alan</u> will attend Yale in the fall.

3. Children taking violin lessons often enjoy playing "<u>Twinkle, Twinkle, Little Star</u>," a piece known throughout France as a famous children's folk song.

4. I always look forward to driving on <u>Highway 1, a road</u> (with spectacular ocean views.)

5. <u>San Francisco, a city</u> built on seven hills, reminds many people of Rome.

6. On the poster, which was cracked and peeling off the brown bricks, he read the name of <u>Don Manuel Garcia, the famous flamenco dancer</u> from Granada, Spain.

7. All the guests sat patiently waiting for <u>Wanda's famous dessert</u>, the best apple pie in the whole village of Wola Mielecka.

8. a. <u>Chunk Cartelli, author</u> of "Pasta and More," ...

   b. "<u>Pasta and More</u>," one of the best books ...

9. One of his heroes was <u>Scott Joplin, composer</u> of hundreds of lovely rag-time piano pieces that have been popular since the end of the nineteenth century.

10. In <u>the wild west, the frontier of the young United States,</u> women were scarce and schooling was usually at a bare minimum.

Practice 10: Nouns

1. The pool <u>water</u> was a constant 80 degrees fahrenheit.

ANSWERS

2. Our <u>math</u> <u>teacher</u> was so nervous about his <u>class</u> <u>observation</u> that he left his <u>lesson</u> <u>plan</u> at home.

3. It seems that <u>soda</u> <u>machine</u> works better after a firm kick.

4. Two fat hens and one colorful rooster raced around the <u>chicken</u> <u>coop</u> squawking and scratching.

5. During the course of the weekly <u>budget</u> <u>meeting</u>, Mr. Chen, the financial counselor assigned to our unit, offered some important suggestions about our company's <u>money</u> <u>management.</u>

6. She flung her <u>pencil</u> <u>case</u> at the door in anger, but her older brother slipped out just in time.

7. The <u>plant</u> <u>holder</u> came equipped with a black light to enhance growth and an <u>instruction</u> <u>booklet</u> that explained the use of the unusual light.

8. On the neat wooden table sat a <u>ceramic</u> <u>cookie</u> <u>jar</u> full of aromatic cookies, and a matching <u>sugar</u> <u>bowl</u> and creamer.

9. <u>Watermelon</u> <u>rinds</u> lay all over the <u>kitchen</u> <u>counter</u>, and seeds were strewn across the shiny <u>linoleum</u> <u>floor</u>, glistening wet and impossible to pick up.

10. When they arrived at their hotel, the company had sent a <u>fruit</u> <u>basket</u> and some cut flowers to welcome them to their temporary home.

Practice 11: Articles

1. All of <u>the</u> new diskettes have been put in <u>a</u> box labeled "Diskettes - New" on top of <u>the</u> Main Counter.

2. If any of <u>the</u> ingredients are left out, <u>the</u> result will be <u>a</u> sticky, awful-tasting mess.

3. Before leaving for <u>the</u> beach, be sure you have your bathing suit, <u>a</u> beach towel, at least one good book, and <u>a</u> sandwich or <u>a</u> snack.

4. He sat on the musem bench, staring at the huge, overpowering painting, awed by the colors and the sense of urgency they created.

5. English 52 is already filled, but by the time you go to register, they might have opened up a new class or two.

Practice 12: Pronouns

1. Henry fully intended to let them know of his decision, but
   (3rd, pl, obj)

   by the time he'd made up his mind to go tell someone in the
   (3rd, sing, sub)   (indef. obj)

   office, they'd all gone home.
   (3rd, pl, sub)

2. It's important that you study critically everything
   (Impers)   (2nd, s or pl; s)   (Indef. obj)

   I teach you in this class; you're not here to meekly
   (1st pers sing., sub) (2nd pers, obj) (2nd pers. sub)

   accept what is given, but to question it.
   (Indef. obj.)   (3rd pers. sing. obj)

3. You tell someone and he tells someone else, and that's how
   (2nd pers, sub) (indef. obj.) (3rd pers, sub) (indef. obj.)   (Impers. sub.)

   gossip travels.

4. Who knows what he   or   she really wants in this life?
   (inter sub)   (3rd pers, sub) (3rd pers, sub)

5. The ones in the red bin cost $1.50, and those over there, on
   (indef.)   (demonst. sub.)

   the counter, cost $2.00; which would you like?
                                        (2nd, p.s., or p; sub)

6. Did you see that?   He sawed his assistant in half,
   (2nd, sub) (demonst. obj.) (3rd, sing, sub)

   and then she got up and did it to   him.
   (3rd, sing, sub)   (impers obj) (3rd p.s., obj)

7. They quizzed each other on what they'd learned in class
   (3rd p.s., sub)   (recip obj)   (3rd p. pl., sub)

   that day.

8. Don't put that there, it's too heavy.
   (demonst. obj.) (3rd p.s., sub)

9. <u>No one</u> could possibly have guessed <u>what</u>   <u>he</u>'d had in
  (indef. sub)   (impers. obj) (3rd ps.s, sub)

   mind when <u>he</u> gathered <u>them</u> together.
         (3rd p.s., sub) (3rd p. pl., obj)

10. <u>We</u> need to think of <u>ourselves</u> sometimes, to the exclusion
(1st p.pl., sub)   (reflexive, obj.)

   of all <u>others</u>, because <u>nobody</u> else really knows what <u>we</u> need.
      (indef. obj)   (indef. sub)   (1st p.pl., sub)

Practice 13: Adjective

1. The <u>scribbled</u> note was almost <u>impossible</u> to read, even with
     (Part A)   (A)

   her <u>powerful</u> <u>magnifying</u> glass.
      (A)   (G)

2. <u>Crushed</u> or <u>dried</u> garlic will do in <u>this</u> recipe, but <u>chopped</u>,
 (Part A)   (Part A)   (DA)   (Part A)

   <u>fresh</u> garlic is much better.
   (A)

3. What did you do with that <u>aluminium</u> foil I bought at the <u>new</u>
                   (AN)   (A)

   supermarket <u>this</u> morning?
         (DA)

4. <u>Flying</u> squirrels are not often seen around here, but if you're
   (G)

   <u>patient</u>, you might get to see the <u>tree</u> squirrel that often plays
   (A)   (AN)

   around that <u>big</u> tree over there.
        (A)

5. The <u>earthenware</u> bowl, <u>dripping</u> with <u>melted</u> chocolate, sat
     (AN)   (G)   (Part A)

   in the sink waiting to be washed, but before she ran the water
   into it, her <u>two</u> children dipped <u>their</u> hands into it and licked
         (A)   (PA)

   all the chocolate off the edges.

6. Karl had already talked to <u>his</u> landlady, and the <u>same</u>
              (PA)   (A)

detective that had been there yesterday was planning on a
repeat visit this afternoon, unaware of Karl's plan.
   (A) .   (DA)   (A)   (PA)

7. To prepare for her demonstration of the winning   original
                  (PA)   (G)   (A)
   recipe, she assembled carefully all the necessary ingredients:
                                        (A)
   sliced green peppers and eggplant, chopped celery, several
   (Part A)   (Part A)   (A)
   tomatoes cut up, a diced onion, grated garlic, and some cheese
          (Part A) (Part A)   (Part A)   (A)
   she'd already grated beforehand.

8. During the wedding, crying babies and fidgeting children
                    (G)   (G)
   distracted everyone from concentrating on the beautiful
                                        (A)
   ceremony, but the bride was truly delighted that all the young
                           (Part A)   (A)
   children in the large family were able to be there for her
             (A)   (A)
   special day, and to her the crying was delightful music.
   (A)   (A)

9. A stranger little brown bird perched on the highest branch,
     (A)   (A)   (A)   (A)
   singing a lively song that Giuseppe had never heard in all his
         (A)
   young life.
   (A)

10. Plaintive and reed-like, the sounds of the bag-pipe sliced
    (A)   (A)
   through the evening calm, piercing in quality, reminding Sean
          (AN)   (G)
   of his summers in the highlands.

Practice 14: Adverbs

1. Do your work as well and as quickly as you can.
2. Internet allows you to communicate globally from your own
   home computer.

3. She laughed <u>loudly</u> and <u>wholeheartedly</u>, and the infectious sound <u>soon</u> had the whole roomful of nervous students giggling.

4. The brownies disappeared <u>faster</u> than any other dessert on the table, and Maria rushed back and forth to the kitchen with the tray, replenishing the ever-dwindling supply.

5. <u>Ordinarily</u> we don't meet so <u>often</u>, but the project we're <u>currently</u> working on is more complex and seems to require our getting together more <u>frequently.</u>

6. The folding chairs were all stacked <u>precariously</u>, forming a very unstable tower of black and beige.

7. He swallowed <u>drily</u> and took two steps backward, until he felt the cold, brick wall against his back.

8. The door clanged shut <u>heavily</u>, echoing <u>weirdly</u> through the large, barn-like room like a metallic thunder-clap.

9. The youth grabbed <u>wildly</u> at the branches that hung out over the rushing river, gasping <u>fiercely</u> for air and screaming for help.

10. "Get out!" she yelled <u>sharply</u>, picking up a book and hurling it <u>viciously</u> at his head.

Practice 15: Adjectives and Adverbs

1. He answered <u>timidly</u>, but his answer was <u>correct</u>.
                (Adv)   (Adj)

2. Your <u>youngest</u> son is <u>quite</u> <u>tall</u> for his age.
          (Adj)   (Adv) (Adj)

3. The <u>stupid</u> computer's <u>broken</u> <u>again</u>!
       (Adj)   (Adj)   (Adv)

4. The <u>silver</u> key goes to the <u>red</u> car, but the <u>other</u> one is <u>very</u>
        (Adj)   (Adj)   (Adj)   (Adv)
   <u>old</u> and serves <u>no</u> <u>useful</u> purpose.
   (Adj)   (Adv) (Adj)

5. Stir the garlic and butter <u>quickly</u> as you add the vegetables,
                            (Adv)
   so that they don't get <u>too</u> <u>hot</u> <u>too</u> <u>fast</u>.
                    (Adv) (Adj) (Adv) (Adj)

6. In the black box she found a small ring, whose stones
      (Adj)   (Adj)   (Adj)
   glowed brightly under the strong lamp.
          (Adv)   (Adj)

7. The speaker pointed importantly at the boring charts he'd
                  (Adv)   (Adj)
   brought, and a loud snore suddenly broke the heavy tension
              (Adj)   (Adv)   (Adj)
   in the room.

8. Seated at her window, Séverine could faintly hear the
  (Adj)   (Adv)
   mournful, haunting chords of a Chopin nocturne, played
    (Adj)   (Adj)   (Adj)
   slowly and with extraordinary depth of feeling.
   (Adv)   (Adj)

9. She hinted vaguely that she was too tired to continue.
         (Adv)   (Adv) (Adj)

10. The cake rose fast in the hot oven, golden and fragrant,
          (Adv)   (Adj)   (Adj)   (Adj)
    and Claudia removed it quickly, gently closing the oven
                  (Adv)   (Adv)   (Adj)
    door with her foot.
         (Adj)

Practice 16: Prepositions

1. This letter should be forwarded to the payroll office, with the appropriate forms.

2. The information was faxed to our office by the president pro tem, indicating to all concerned that they were to continue following the usual procedure but that all memos would now be routed through the secretary's office.

3. He ran through the doorway and dashed up the stairs, calling to his friend as he ran.

4. Everywhere she looked there were clothes—on every table, under the chairs, draped across the couch, even hanging over the lamp.

5. Brilliant sunlight streamed through the window, slashed into blinding slices by the Venetian blinds, illuminating tiny, dancing motes of dust.

6. She wrote the sentence <u>on</u> the blackboard, drawing a line <u>under</u> all the prepositions.

7. Darting and weaving, the kittens ran <u>around</u> the bush and climbed <u>up</u> the tree, jumping <u>from</u> branch <u>to</u> branch until they finally leapt <u>onto</u> the roof <u>of</u> the garage.

8. Holding the envelope <u>to</u> the light, Benoit tried to discern the amount <u>on</u> the line and the signature scrawled <u>across</u> the bottom.

9. She stopped typing, hands poised <u>over</u> the keyboard, and listened again <u>for</u> the faint sound, her heart thumping wildly <u>against</u> her chest.

10. Clementine's ball <u>of</u> yarn rolled <u>off</u> her lap, bounced <u>against</u> the bag that was propped <u>up</u> at her feet, and continued rolling slowly <u>out</u> the open door and <u>onto</u> the landing.

Practice 17: Conjunctions

1. <u>If</u> you ever need help, don't hesitate to call <u>and</u> we'll send someone right away.
2. Let us know <u>when</u> you get there, <u>and</u> we'll send a car to meet you.
3. <u>Either</u> they take the offer we made them, <u>or</u> we just forget about the whole deal.
4. Take it <u>or</u> leave it!
5. In a mixture of this sort, the results can be quite surprising; <u>therefore,</u> I must stress again that everyone using the lab today must wear protective goggles.
6. They didn't take <u>either</u> the money <u>or</u> the food we left them, <u>but</u> I bet they took <u>both</u> the radio <u>and</u> the car keys.
7. Whales are mammals, like humans, <u>and</u> <u>although</u> they live in water, they breathe air; <u>moreover,</u> they bear their young ones <u>and</u> produce milk to feed them.
8. In 1998, <u>if</u> all goes well, my brother will finish college, <u>but</u> he plans on going a fifth year to graduate school <u>while</u> he looks for jobs in his field.
9. <u>Since</u> I haven't finished the manuscript yet, the printer can't begin his work <u>and</u> the typographer will have to work overtime all next week.
10. The sauce isn't ready yet, <u>so</u> don't boil the spaghetti yet.

ANSWERS

Practice 18: Roots and Affixes

1. -scrib — write
2. oper- — work
3. -struct — build, pile up
4. -cend — ash, burn
5. -vis, vid — separate
6. -luc — light
7. -port — carry
8. -nutri — to suckle
9. -centr — center
10. -ten — hold
11. -dict — say
12. run- — move
13. -rect — straight, right
14. -equi — equal, same
15. -frig — cold
16. -tent — hold
17. vend- — sell
18. bake — cook
19. -stud — study
20. -cip — take

Practice 19: More Fun with Roots and Affixes...

1. duc- — lead
2. min — to jut out
3. -flam — flame, burn
4. -cid — kill
5. -candesc — to glow, shine
6. -muni — city
7. -nasc — be born
8. cogni — know
9. spati — space
10. abund — to overflow
11. techno — art, craft
12. -vit — life
13. -tract — pull
14. -critic — judge, discern
15. -nounce — report
16. approb — approve
17. carto — map, chart
18. -cant — sing
19. chrono — time
20. rad — root

Practice 20: Prefixes

1. auto - self
2. poly - many; un- not
3. synth - together
4. anti - against
5. re - again
6. un - not
7. anti - against
8. ante - before
9. con - with
10. en - to bring about, cause to be
11. un - not
12. micro - very small
13. bio - life
14. patri - father
15. retro - backward
16. multi - many
17. de - not
18. ethno - race, people
19. ex - out of
20. trans - across, through

Practice 21: Suffixes

1. ian - one who
11. al - adjective ending

2. *ly* - adverb ending
3. *ant* - adjective ending
4. *y* - adjective ending
5. *ion* - noun ending
6. *ful* - full of

7. *ite* - adjective ending
8. *ator, -or* - that which, one who
9. *al* - adjective ending
10. *ive* - adjective ending

12. *cide* - kill
13. *ial* - adjective ending
14. *ence* - noun ending
15. *or* - that which, one who
16. *ism* - doctrine, theory, practice
17. *hibit* - hold
18. *ous* - adjective ending
19. *ible* - able
20. *ment* - noun ending

Practice 22: Roots and Affixes

1. desper/ation
2. re/act/ion/ary
3. mis/anthrop/y
4. pre/nat/al
5. contra/cept/ive
6. auto/mot/ive
7. sequel
8. re/make
9. arbor/eal
10. avia/tion
11. micro/organ/ism
12. counter/pro/duct/ive
13. trans/port/ation
14. com/pell/ing
15. serr/ate/d
16. de/tach/able
17. mis/inform/ed
18. tele/scop/ic
19. in/com/prehens/ible
20. anti/dis/establish/ment/arian/ism

Practice 23: Word Families

1. curiosity
2. tenacious
3. marry
4. infinitely
5. misfortune
6. monstrous
7. enable
8. derivative, derivation
9. musically
10. tighten

Practice 24: Verbs

1. If you're really quick, you can see the coyote as it comes
       C   T/A   T/A
   around that outcropping.
2. The old carpet had been used for so many years that the floor
                          T/P
   boards could be seen in a line from one door to the other.
       T/P

ANSWERS

3. Her grandson <u>climbed</u> up on her lap, <u>threw</u> his arms around
     T/A   T/A
 her neck, and <u>grinned</u> mischievously.
      T/A

4. Flags <u>flapped</u> in the breeze as fireworks <u>exploded</u> high over
    T/A   T/A
 the lake.

5. The water for the noodles <u>was boiling</u> over, but as he <u>reached</u>
         T/A   T/A
 for the lid, the pot-holder he <u>was holding</u> <u>was pulled</u> out of
          T/A   T/P
 his grip when it <u>snagged</u> on another pot handle.
       T/A

6. It <u>fell</u> into the pot of sauce, and as it <u>hit</u> with a loud splat,
  T/A   T/A
 orange-colored sauce <u>splattered</u> all over the counter and the
        T/A
 floor.

7. The boy <u>took</u> aim, <u>closed</u> one eye and <u>pulled</u> the trigger; one
    T/A   T/A   T/A
 duck <u>was clearly hit</u>, and another <u>began</u> to fall but <u>pulled back</u>
    T/P   T/A   T/A
 out of its dive and <u>continued</u> flying.
        T/A

8. If you <u>submit</u> the application by Friday, there<u>'s</u> still time; it
    T/A   C
 <u>can be processed</u> by Admissions next week, and you
   T/P
 <u>should be informed</u> of their decision by the Registrar in early
   T/P
 January.

9. By the end of this school year, Marius <u>will have been</u> in this
                C
 country for over a year.

10. My teacher's <u>been honored</u> with an award for excellent
      T/P

teaching, and I <u>heard</u> that a wonderful speech <u>was given</u> by
            T/A   T/P

the President of the college at the awards ceremony.

Practice 25: Verbs

1. When <u>parking</u> on a hill, it's important <u>to engage</u> the parking
           G   I

   brake and <u>to turn</u> the wheels toward the curb.
         I

2. <u>Honking</u> and <u>flapping</u> their wings, the gaggle of geese ran
    G   G

   after the unknown visitor, forcing him <u>to turn and run</u> back
                                    I

   towards the woods and <u>abandon</u> all hope of <u>approaching</u> the
                      I   G

   house.

3. Don't blame me if you forget to <u>turn off</u> the power and there's
                                I

   a short circuit.

4. When she was little, she learned <u>to play</u> the accordion and
                                I

   the piano, and now whenever they're <u>having</u> a party at the
                                    G

   dorm, they call on her to <u>play and liven</u> things up.
                                I

5. If you insist on <u>doing</u> it yourself, at least let me give you
               G

   some pointers on <u>avoiding</u> mishaps.
             G

6. Before <u>adding</u> the flour to the banana mixture, pour a few
          G

   drops of vinegar into a third of a cup of milk (<u>to make</u> it
                                   I

   sour), and let it sit while you continue <u>adding</u> the other
                                  G

   ingredients.

7. As soon as class was finished, the two friends went <u>swimming</u>
                                           G

ANSWERS

in their favorite <u>swimming</u> hole, but since they forgot <u>to bring</u>
               G   I

towels, they dried off by <u>chasing</u> each other around the
                                 G

water's edge.

8. <u>Cooking</u> can be very <u>relaxing</u>, especially if you have a good
    G   G

friend <u>to help</u> you eat the results.
       I

9. If you enjoy <u>snorkeling</u>, you have <u>to visit</u> the Great Barrier
               G   I

Reef off Australia, which offers some of the best fish <u>viewing</u>
                                            G

in the world.

10. After <u>drifting</u>, unsure and unsettled, for so many years, Oskar
      G

finally decided <u>to settle</u> down, <u>to finish</u> his studies, and
                  I   I

<u>to find</u> himself a good woman <u>to share</u> the rest of his life
  I   I
with.

Practice 26: Verbs

1. "<u>Have</u> you ever <u>tasted</u> vanilla-flavored tea?" She <u>asked</u> her
   aux   main   main

guests as she <u>put</u> the kettle on.
              main

2. The sled <u>was</u> <u>flying</u> downhill faster, faster, picking up speed
           aux   main

as it <u>sped</u> past trees and rocks, and soon it <u>was</u> <u>heading</u> for
     main   aux   main

the fence that <u>surrounded</u> the parking area at the bottom of
              main

the hill.

3. If you <u>had</u> never <u>seen</u> the sign, I <u>could</u> <u>understand</u> your
      aux   main   aux   main

actions, but you <u>knew</u> it <u>was</u> there as well as I <u>did</u>.
             main   main   aux

4. I <u>thought</u> they <u>would</u> <u>have</u> already <u>finished</u> priming and
main   aux   aux   main

   painting the whole exterior by now, but as it <u>turns</u> out, they
                                                  main

   <u>haven't</u> even <u>started</u> painting yet.
     aux   main

5. Even though she <u>can</u> hardly <u>afford</u> food and clothes for all
                  aux   main

   her kids, she'<u>s</u> <u>planning</u> on buying a computer so she <u>can</u>
            aux   main   aux

   <u>start</u> a business at home.
   main

6. You <u>haven't</u> <u>lived</u> until you'<u>ve</u> <u>skied</u> in the Alps!
      aux   main   aux main

7. Once you'<u>ve</u> <u>added</u> the spices and the sauce <u>is</u> <u>bubbling</u>,
      aux   main   aux   main

   you <u>don't</u> <u>want</u> to forget to keep stirring.
      aux   main

8. Antonia <u>had</u> never <u>heard</u> a mandolin until she <u>visited</u> her
        aux   main   main

   grandparents in Naples.

9. Just about everyone in the class <u>has</u> already <u>had</u> the
                            aux   main

   chickenpox, but I'm not sure if the teacher'<u>s</u> <u>had</u> it.
                                 aux main

10. He <u>didn't</u> <u>do</u> it! I <u>saw</u> the whole thing, and just like I'<u>ve</u>
     aux main   main   aux

   <u>told</u> the police, he <u>didn't</u> <u>do</u> any of what they <u>say</u> he'<u>s</u> <u>done</u>!
   main   aux main   main   aux main

Practice 27: Verbs

1. boils - simple present indicative
2. come - simple present indicative
3. were - simple past subjunctive; 'd (would) buy - conditional;
   's (has) wanted - present perfect indicative
4. had ..... tasted - pluperfect indicative
5. Get - present imperative; get - present imperative
6. are - simple present indicative; 've (have) heard ... seen - present
   perfect indicative; are - simple present indicative; hope - simple present
   indicative; will have done - future perfect indicative.

7. don't mind -simple present indicative; let - present imperative
8. remind - simple present indicative; is - simple present indicative; get - present subjunctive; are (signed) - simple present indicative.
9. was playing - past progressive (continuous) indicative; lost - simple past indicative; was - simple past indicative;
10. could get along - simple past subjunctive

Practice 28: Verbs

1. They <u>couldn't</u> stay awake while they studied, so they decided they <u>would</u> make a pot of coffee.
2. "You <u>ought</u> to do it up right," he drawled, before spitting in the sand.
3. He <u>can't</u> afford his car payments, so he definitely <u>shouldn't</u> plan on taking a vacation this year.
4. Nutrition experts agree that Americans <u>should</u> eat less red meat, and I think everyone here <u>must</u> agree that we <u>should</u> certainly cut back on salty junk food.
5. "<u>Can</u> I go, Mommy, please, <u>can</u> I, <u>can</u> I?"
"<u>May</u> I. You know you <u>should</u> say 'May I' when you're asking permission.
6. Many people feel that the government <u>ought</u> to be less involved in our lives, my husband believes it <u>should</u> be more involved but in fewer areas.
7. <u>Can</u> you play the piano?
8. So let's get started now, <u>shall</u> we?
9. If she thinks I <u>shouldn't</u> put so much salt in the food I cook, in my house, then she <u>should</u> stay home and cook her own food!
10. The announcer on the radio said we <u>might</u> have a storm this evening, but it looks as if it <u>may</u> start raining sooner than that.

Practice 29 : Verbs

1. <u>Crack</u> the eggs with care, and if any of the shell <u>falls</u> in,
   T   I
<u>remove</u> it carefully.
  T

2. He <u>said</u> he <u>wanted</u> to take a shower before leaving the house.
    T   T

3. He <u>said</u> he'<u>s</u> a cowboy, and that he <u>breaks</u> horses for a ranch ·
    T   I   T
   about fifty miles from here.

4. "I <u>came</u>, I <u>saw</u>, I <u>conquered</u>" <u>is</u> a famous quote attributed
        I   I   I   I
   to Julius Caesar.

5. Francesco never <u>eats</u> lasagna, but he'<u>s</u> crazy about cannelloni.
               T   I

6. Publishing <u>is</u> a time-consuming business that <u>requires</u> long
           I   T
   hours, intense dedication and lots of imagination and up-front
   money.

7. If you <u>intend</u> to prepare the whole dinner yourself, <u>get</u> an
         I   T
   apron and <u>go</u> to it.
           I

8. When we'<u>re</u> in kindergarten, we <u>learn</u> to listen to those older
          I   T
   than us, to hold hands, to tell the truth, and to share; all in
   all, that'<u>s</u> not bad advice for us older folks to take to heart,
          I
   too.

9. The sound of horses' hooves <u>thundered</u> across the prairie, and
                            I
   the herd <u>kicked up</u> a dust storm that <u>was</u> visible for miles
            T   I
   in each direction

10. My son <u>loves</u> computer games, and <u>can spend</u> hours at them;
        T   T
    my daughter, on the other hand, <u>is</u> perfectly content to sit
                               I
    with a good book for hour after hour.

PART III

Practice 30: Phrases and Clauses

1. P	3. C	5. P	7. P	9. C
2. C	4. C	6. C	8. P	10. P

ANSWERS

Practice 31: Phrases and Clauses

1. Do this <u>for me:</u> put <u>your name</u> at the top of the page, look
         prep   noun   prep   prep
  <u>at the test paper</u> (OR: <u>look at</u> <u>the test paper</u>), and decide
      prep   verb phr.   noun
  <u>how much</u> of it you <u>can answer</u> with certainty.
    noun   prep   verb Phr.   prep

2. <u>The PTA</u> <u>were excited</u> <u>at the opportunity</u> to have
     noun   verb   prep
  <u>a real, live author</u> come talk <u>to the classes.</u>
        noun   prep

3. Bugs covered <u>the outside</u> of the screen, making <u>rasping noises</u>
               noun   prep   noun
  that Jill found irritating.

4. He played <u>all kinds</u> of music <u>on only a saw and a comb,</u> and
           noun   prep   prep
  <u>his audience</u> was enthralled <u>by it.</u>
    noun   prep

5. <u>The orchestra</u> played music <u>of Tchaikovsky and Beethoven,</u>
     noun   prep
  and ended <u>their outdoor concert</u> <u>with a rousing rendition</u>
             noun   prep
  <u>of Handel's Royal Fireworks Music</u> accompanied
              prep
  <u>by real fireworks.</u>
      prep

6. <u>The two little boys</u> rolled <u>down the same grassy hill,</u>
        noun   prep
  <u>over and over,</u> tumbling <u>over each other</u>
     adv   prep
  (OR: <u>tumbling over each other</u>) and <u>rolling head over heels,</u>
        gerund   gerund
  and when they tried <u>to stand up</u> they were <u>so dizzy</u> that they
                 Inf   adj
  <u>fell back down,</u> <u>clutching the ground</u> and
    verb   gerund
  <u>laughing until their sides hurt</u> (OR: <u>until their sides hurt</u>).
       gerund   prep

7. Mai Yee stopped eating, <u>her chopsticks</u> poised <u>in the air,</u> and
                            noun   prep
  <u>without a sound</u> she rose <u>from her seat</u> <u>by the window</u> and
   prep   prep   prep
  sped <u>to the door</u> to intercept <u>the messenger</u>
        prep   noun
  (OR: <u>to intercept the messenger</u>).
       Inf

8. Once <u>the mayonnaise</u> is added <u>to the sauce,</u> <u>the rest</u>
        noun   prep   noun
  <u>of the ingredients</u> <u>have to be added</u> immediately, or
    prep   verb
  <u>the whole mixture</u> <u>will soon begin</u> <u>to turn into</u>
    noun   verb   Inf
  <u>a brown, gooey mess</u> (OR: <u>into a brown gooey mess</u>).
     noun   prep

9. <u>Buying his first car</u> (OR: <u>his first car</u>) was <u>the beginning</u>
    gerund   noun   noun
  <u>of John's new life</u> <u>of independence.</u>
    prep   prep

10. Her goal was <u>to be the best darned first-grade teacher</u>
                  Inf
  (OR: <u>the best darned first-grade teacher</u>)
            noun
  that Clanton, Mississippi had <u>ever seen.</u>
                     verb

Practice 32: Phrases and Clauses

1. <u>The books</u> <u>we borrowed yesterday</u> had to be returned to the library by March first.
2. <u>Chicken is one type of meat</u> <u>that must be kept well chilled until use.</u>
3. <u>My kids won't eat any sauce</u> <u>that has vegetable in it.</u>
4. Generally speaking, <u>kids</u> <u>who are expected to do well in school by their parents</u> usually wind up doing just that.
5. <u>Mr. Ashkenazy plays Rachmaninoff with a depth of expression</u> <u>that I've never heard before in a pianist.</u>

6. When the rice mixture <u>that's browning in the pan</u> begins to sizzle, pour in the water <u>I've already measured into the cup</u> over there.

7. <u>Old-Faithful is a geyser in Yellowstone National Park</u> <u>that erupts once every hour</u>.

8. <u>Although all his colleagues defended cases</u> <u>that brought them</u> <u>bundles of money and renown</u>, <u>Jake always preferred</u> <u>representing people in court</u> <u>who otherwise could never afford</u> <u>a decent lawyer</u>.

9. <u>In her whole life she'd never seen such a mess; everywhere</u> <u>she looked there were piles of stuff, mountains of junk</u> <u>he'd</u> <u>probably never use and probably didn't even know was there</u>.

10. <u>Eyes closed as if in prayer, Agniezka was lost</u> <u>in the amazing</u> <u>variations of sounds</u> <u>she was able to produce on the ancient</u> <u>organ</u>.

Practice 33: Phrases and Clauses

1) **Prepositional phrases:** below Mount Fuji / between its plain and the rugged sea / of Numazu / at the convergence / of three fault lines / In this town / of a thousand pines / with her daughter, Claudia / from their little apartment / near the railroad tracks / to the tiny road / up the mountain / at the little stone shrine / in small vases / next to it / up the winding road / at the sight / of the funny hens and noisy roosters / next to the pagoda / on the slide / in the little playground / after visiting the pagoda / down the mountain.

2) **Independent Clauses:** sits the town of Numazu / It lies at the convergence of three fault lines, and often shakes / Marcella lived with her daughter, Claudia / they walked from their little apartment near the railroad tracks to the tiny road that led up the mountain called Kanukiyama / they would stop at the little stone shrine/ Claudia enjoyed the colorful flowers / Then they would walk, slowly, slowly, up the winding road, stopping / Marcella knew they were there / Each time, they spent at least an hour playing on the slide in the little playground / and then, after visiting the pagoda, they began their slow walk back down the mountain.

3. **Dependent Clauses :** as the earth struggles to release its pressure / that led up the mountain called Kanukiyama / As they began their ascent / that someone always kept in small vases next to it / only once they'd reached the old pagoda / When Claudia squealed at the sight of the funny hens and noisy roosters / that lived next to the pagoda.

PART IV

Practice 34 : Sentences

1. <u>You</u> <u>want</u> to come with us to the beach.
    S   V

2. <u>They</u> <u>are speaking</u> in English language.
    S   V

3. <u>You</u> <u>have never heard</u> of comparative linguistics.
    S   V

4. <u>You</u> <u>said</u> that <u>the report</u> <u>won't be ready</u> until Friday.
    S   V   S   V

5. <u>Those cookies</u> <u>are</u> for someone in particular.
       S   V

6. <u>Your Dad</u> <u>is coming</u> to the Father-Daughter Dance with you
     S   V

 or <u>he</u> <u>is going</u> to be out of town.
     S   V

7. <u>You</u> <u>think</u> <u>they</u> <u>meant</u> what they said.
    S   V   S   V

8. <u>They</u> <u>won't ever change</u> their minds.
    S   V

9. <u>She</u> <u>hasn't seen</u> that movie already.
    S   V

10. <u>You</u> <u>have</u> (some) game programs on your computer at home.
     S   V

Practice 35: Sentences

1. S	3. C	5. C	7. C	9. S
2. S	4. Cx	6. C-Cx	8. S	10. C-Cx

Practice 36: Sentences

1. Imp   3. I   5. I with embedded S clause   7. S   9. I
2. I   4. S   6. I   8. I   10. I

PART V

Practice 37: Punctuation

1. "Hey, you!" cried the shopkeeper, "come back here!"

2. In her class on world literature, she studied works by Chekov, Shakespeare, Twain(,) and Zola.

3. If they dont' have garlic, just buy the onions and the oregano.

4. Mrs. Chiang's neighbours always barbecued on Fridays, and once in a while(,) when they didn't have too many people over(,) they asked her to join them.

5. A marsupial is an animal that carries its young in a pouch; they're almost all indigenous to Australia, although North America has one: the opossum. (OR: ...pouch. They're...)

6. The Sousaphone, a variation of the tuba, was named for John Phillip Sousa, a world-famous American composer of marches.

7. Picture this: six open-topped train cars in a row, each one with a giraffe's head (a real one) sticking out the top.
   (OR: ... head—a real one-sticking ...)

8. In order to prepare for his university year abroad, Andrew made sure he had a passport, two pairs of solid walking shoes, an umbrella, and gifts for his host family.

9. If you want to invent a new recipe, you have to be absolutely sure what each of the ingredients does; if not, you can wind up with something quite different from what you had in mind.

10. My mother-in-law's driving is awful; her rapidly-failing vision makes her reaction time dangerously slow.

Practice 38: Punctuation

How important were the missions to California? Open up a map. Those words may look like city names, but before there was a city there, the name was already in place, from Basilica

San Diego de Alcala in the south all the way up past San Francisco de Asis — and a few more along the way: Santa Barbara, San Luis Obispo. Is there a big city missing? Not really. Before it became the City of the Angels, Los Angeles belonged to an archangel, San Gabriel, and the mission named for him sat at the crossroads of the west coast of America.

PART VI

Practice 39: Spelling

1. VCCV	6. VCV	11. VCV	16. VCV
2. VCV	7. VCCV	12. VCV	17. VCV
3. VCCV	8. VCV	13. VCCV	18. VCCV
4. VCCV	9. VCV	14. VCCV	19. VCCV
5. VCCV	10. VCV	15. VCCV	20. VCV

Practice 40: Spelling

1. flying	11. reviewing
2. whining	12. abutting
3. siding	13. whittling
4. swimming	14. shunning
5. jogging	15. communing
6. whipping	16. batting
7. thrilling	17. judging
8. revealing	18. timing
9. donning	19. persuing
10. slicing	20. imitating

Further Reading ...

Adventures of a Verbivore, by Richard Lederer, 1994. Simon & Schuster, Inc., New York. A rollicking good time with words.

American Heritage College Dictionary. Houghton, Mifflin Company, Boston.

Better Spelling, by James I. Brown and Thomas E. Pearsall, 1992. D.C. Heath and Company, Lexington, Massachusetts. Test your spelling competence, learn your weaknesses and improve them. Lots of exercises.

Crazy English, by Richard Lederer, 1994. Simon &.. Schuster. Inc., New York. Another rollicking good time with words.

Good Grief, Good Grammar, by Dianna Booher, 1988. Ballantine Books, New York. Its subtitle says it all: the Business Person's Guide to Grammar and Usage.

Grammar for Smart People, by Barry Tarshis, 1992. Simon &. Schuster, Inc., New York.

Handbook for Writers, by Lynn Quitman Troyka, 1987. Prentice Hall, Inc., Englewood Cliffs, NJ·

How to Achieve Competence In English, by Eric W. Johnson, 1991. Bantam Books, New York. An alphabetical listing of grammar topics explained succinctly.

Mother Tongue, The, by Bill Bryson, 1990. William Morrow and Co., Inc., New York.

Pocket Style Manual, by Diana Hacker, 1993. Bedford Books of St. Martin's Press, Boston. Small, portable, succinct, a quick reference for writers and researchers.

St. Martin's Handbook, The, by Andrea Lunsford and Robert Connors. St. Martin's Press, New York, 1992. Complete English grammar for serious study.

Strictly Speaking, by Edwin Newman. Warner Books, 1974. **The** amazing mis-uses of English.

Webster's New Universal Unabridged Dictionary, Deluxe Edition. Simon and Schuster, New York. A hefty book for real word-lovers.

Webster's New World Dictionary of the American **Language.** The World Publishing Company.

Webster's New World Dictionary, Popular Library Pocket-Size Edition. The World Publishing company. Small enough to go anywhere with you.

INDEX